FREDERICK
IN THE
CIVIL WAR

FREDERICK
IN THE
CIVIL WAR

Battle & Honor in the Spired City

JOHN W. SCHILDT

THE
History
PRESS

Published by The History Press
Charleston, SC 29403
www.historypress.net

Cover images: Harper's Weekly; Generals Early and Wallace. *Library of Congress*; Frederick
County Tourism.

First published 2010
Second printing 2014

Manufactured in the United States

ISBN 978.1.60949.078.2

Schildt, John W.
Frederick in the Civil War : battle and honor in the spired city / John W. Schildt.
p. cm.
Includes bibliographical references and index.
ISBN 978-1-60949-078-2
1. Frederick (Md.)--History--Civil War, 1861-1865. I. Title.
F189.F8S3 2010
975.2'03--dc22
2010043167

To my aunt, Reba Alice Staley, who early in life shared with me her love and knowledge of Frederick, and to my grandmother, Clara Virginia Hummer Schildt, who saved historical items for me.

CONTENTS

Acknowledgements

A book does not just happen. Years ago, I heard that for every soldier at the battlefront there were twenty in support behind the lines. Thus, I extend my gratitude to Ms. Hannah Cassilly, commissioning editor at The History Press, for suggesting this book and for her guiding hand. And in this day of electronics, Robin Murphy prepared the manuscript and images. Without the assistance of these two ladies, the book would not have made it to print.

The late Judge Edward S. Delaplaine and Glenn H. Worthington wrote extensively on their beloved Frederick. I relied heavily on their writings, as well as the research and writings of the Honorable Paul Gordon, former mayor of Frederick. Likewise John Feisler, director of Frederick County Tourism, and Cathy Bealer, ranger/historian at the Monocacy Battlefield, were most helpful and encouraging, as was Dr. Gordon Dammann of the National Museum of Civil War Medicine.

This book is a product of individuals remembered here, as well as others who through the years have been an inspiration and have been committed to our historical local heritage.

Chapter 1

AT THE CROSSROADS

Centuries ago, wild animals roamed the land, making paths through the wilderness and finding places to ford streams. Native Americans followed the paths that the animals had trod. In central Maryland, according to some traditions, the Susquehanna and Monocacy trails crossed. Eventually, the settlers came to the location and named the site Fredericktown, later Frederick.

The city was begun in 1745. Daniel Dulaney acquired a tract of seven thousand acres. Originally, the area was a part of Prince George's County and was known as Tasker's Chance. Then, in 1745, the site was named Frederick, after Frederick Calvert, the sixth and last Lord Baltimore. The first house was erected by John Thomas Schley. The first child to be born in the new city was Mary Schley. According to tradition, her mother was an Indian squaw. Later, the territory surrounding Frederick became Frederick County, stretching from the Mason-Dixon line in the north to the Potomac River in the south and bounded on the west by Washington County and on the east by Carroll County.

In the early 1700s, settlers began making their way to what we now know as Frederick. Many were Germans, landing near Philadelphia and then traveling westward to Lancaster, York and Hanover. Then they struck the Monocacy trail and migrated to the fertile farmland in what is now Frederick County.

In time, the National Road traversed the land from Baltimore, across the mountains to Hagerstown and beyond. This is now a part of Alternate

The Hessian barracks. *Frederick County Tourism.*

Route 40. Another road, current Route 15, ran north to Gettysburg and Harrisburg and south to Leesburg. There was also the road to Washington, and another, now Route 340, running in a southwesterly direction to Harpers Ferry and the Shenandoah Valley. Thus, Frederick was like the hub of a wheel going out in all directions.

North of Frederick, in the Catoctin Mountains, is Camp David, the presidential retreat and the locale of several summit conferences. However, there was a very important conference in Frederick in 1754. At that time, the French and Indian War was in progress. That year, Benjamin Franklin and General Edward Braddock, commander of His Majesty's forces in the colonies, met in Frederick to plan strategy and consider the logistics of the campaign against the French to the west. At the time, Frederick was on the frontier, and the hinterlands were to the west. There were fewer than two hundred homes, along with several taverns and churches. The construction of a new courthouse was in progress. That came to a halt as the British demanded horses and wagons to assist in hauling supplies for the campaign. The redcoats needed them. The campaign ended in disaster in July. General Braddock was killed, and only the leadership of Colonel Washington saved the army.

Eleven years later, in 1765, twelve judges gathered in Courthouse Square. Meeting on November 23, they repudiated the infamous British

Roger Brookve Taney.
Frederick County Archives.

Stamp Act. This was prior to the Boston Tea Party. The Maryland judges were the first to challenge British rule.

For many years, November 23 was observed as Repudiation Day, honoring the judges who defied George III. A plaque honoring the twelve judges remains at Kemp Hall.

In July 1775, two companies of riflemen from the area made the five-hundred-mile trek to Boston to join the Continental army. A year later, the Maryland legislature decreed that a military post be established in Frederick to accommodate at least two battalions of troops. After they were constructed during 1777–78, the barracks became home to Hessian soldiers captured at the Battle of Saratoga. Later, supplies were stored on the grounds for the Lewis and Clark expedition. During the War

The old Frederick County Courthouse. *Frederick County Archives.*

Between the States, the barracks, located on the grounds of what is now the Maryland School for the Deaf, became an important supply depot for the Union cause, as well as a hospital after the Battles of Antietam and Monocacy. Today, these barracks, containing the history and heritage of the past, remain a very important part of Fredericktown. The structures contain artifacts from the past. There are frequent living history programs on the site, and it is well worth a visit. The barracks are located on South Market Street. Many of the German prisoners were unable to return to their homeland, so they remained in Frederick County and became prosperous farmers in the Middletown Valley, as well as near Utica, north of Frederick.

Near the Frederick County Courthouse was a small white brick building. It housed the law offices of Roger Brooke Taney and Francis Scott Key. Roger Brooke Taney came to Frederick at the urging of Key. There he opened his law office and was introduced to Key's sister, Anne, whom he married on January 7, 1806. Taney and Key did not remain

The supposed location of Taney-Key Law Office. *Author's collection.*

long in Frederick. In 1835, Key was sent by President Andrew Jackson to Alabama to negotiate a settlement between the state and federal governments over the land of the Creek Indians. From 1833 to 1841, Key was the U.S. attorney for the District of Columbia. Key is buried in near the entrance to Frederick's Mount Olivet Cemetery.[1]

In 1831, Taney was appointed by President Andrew Jackson as the attorney general of the United States in 1836. Upon the death of Chief Justice John Marshall, President Jackson appointed Taney to fill that post. Taney remained in that office until his death in 1864.

North of Frederick is Gettysburg, while south of it is Harpers Ferry and the Potomac River. Thus, events far and near influenced happenings in Frederick prior to and during the Civil War. Upon the outbreak of hostilities, Frederick was occupied by Union troops. Three times during the war years, soldiers of the Army of Northern Virginia (Confederate States of America, CSA) entered the city. The Union Army of the Potomac received joyous welcomes in 1862 and 1863 on the roads to Antietam and Gettysburg. In 1864, Frederick paid a $200,000 ransom to Jubal Early's command; just south of the city limits, the Battle of

The Roger Brooke Taney House and Museum. *Frederick County Archives.*

Monocacy, a struggle that perhaps saved the Union, occurred on July 9, 1864. Frederick was indeed at the crossroads of the Civil War.

Years ago, Dr. A. Ross Wentz, writing of the Lutheran church in Frederick, said of the congregation:

> *It is older than the American Republic…it is older than the State of Maryland, older than Frederick County. It has witnessed the entire romance of American history…it has not only witnessed that epic, it has shared in it…it has made its contribution to those who explored, those who colonized, those who founded the American Nation.* [2]

These same comments could be said of Frederick today. Frederick has links to many great American events, and it has links to the Civil War. Frederick stands at the crossroads of history.

Chapter 2

THE GRAPES OF WRATH

G rapes contain seeds. Some grapes taste very good. However, if one eats too many grapes or accidentally swallows some seeds, pain and discomfort will follow.

In the evenings during the 1840s and 1850s, clusters of men sat in village stores and talked. The men of Sharpsburg talked before and after their lodge meetings. They talked of many things, but one issue on their minds was that of the seeds of discontent sweeping across the country.

During these years, there was a variety of reform movements calling for the abolition of slavery. William Lloyd Garrison and, later, Horace Greeley were most outspoken in their demand for immediate freedom of the slaves. Garrison published a newspaper called the *Liberator*. He said that slavery was a covenant with death, an agreement with hell.

The moderate thinkers recognized slavery as an economic and social problem. They saw many problems connected with freedom and realized that there were no easy answers. Slavery must be abolished. Charles Finney, the great evangelist of his day, and Harriet Beecher Stowe were in this group.

As pressure began to mount, the South became more and more defensive. Northern papers were outlawed in many leading cities of the South. Runaway slaves were made out to be public examples. When caught, they were taken to a busy spot in the city and publicly whipped to discourage others from following their example.

There were extremists at each end of the line. Never a majority, these folks were a dynamic minority nonetheless. Speeches and writings

William Nelson Pendleton. *Library of Congress.*

of Garrison, Greeley and Southern congressmen had a profound psychological effect on the nation. The matter of slavery was not allowed to rest. It was kept constantly before the people.

Agricultural developments such as the invention of the McCormick reaper and the great industrial growth of the Northeast played a role in the seeds of discontent. The South did not feel a part of the nation. It seemed as though there were two different societies, two economic systems and two ways of life.

In the South, of course, cotton was king. There was little farming diversity, especially in the Deep South. Slaves were needed to harvest king cotton. After a while, there was a depletion of the soil. The land suffered from the lack of fertilizers and crop rotation.

Complicating matters was the difference between the planters and the plain people. The plain folks on small farms were like the average midwestern farmer, struggling along to make ends meet. On the other hand, the large plantation owners dominated politics, the state government and, to a large extent, even the federal government.

For recreation, both the planters and the average people spent much time riding horseback and in shooting matches. These were to give the South an edge in the early days of the war.

One writer has pictured the seeds of discontent in the South like a totem pole. On top was the plantation owner, with his wealth and acres of land. Next came the small farmer, or poor white farmer, just making

The Kemp Hall plaque.
Frederick County Historical Society.

ends meet, and at the bottom, the slaves. The poor white farmers feared the freedom of the slaves, feeling that then *they* would be on the bottom of the totem pole. But regardless, the North looked—and did not like what it saw. Slavery was wrong, and the press and leaders in the North said so.

The question is often asked, "Was the Civil War inevitable?" For many, the question was not *if* war would come between the North and South, but *when*.

Yearly, whenever new states were admitted to the Union, politicians debated the issue of slavery. The prime movers were three great Americans: John C. Calhoun of South Carolina, Henry Clay of Kentucky and Daniel Webster of Massachusetts. Basically, they sought compromise and appeasement. The reader can research the Missouri Compromise and the Kansas Nebraska Act to further imagine the scenario. Congress aimed to equalize slavery and nonslavery in the new states and draw a western boundary to the problem. Eventually, there was warfare on the Kansas-Missouri border, and John Brown became famous, or infamous, during the Bleeding Kansas years.

Roger Brooke Taney was a dedicated and hardworking jurist. There was never a question as to his loyalty to the United States of America. In 1857, the *Dred Scott* decision came before the Supreme Court. Taney could have selected one of his associates to write the court's decision. However, realizing the controversy of the decision, he wrote the opinion himself. Essentially it said that Dred Scott, an African American, had no rights and was property. The Northern press was appalled, and Taney and the court were greatly criticized. There can be no doubt that the decision fanned the flames of discord and was one of the seeds of wrath that led to the war.[1]

Meanwhile, stations on the Underground Railroad sprang up in Maryland and in the Frederick area. The goal was to help African Americans escape to the North or to Canada. Of course, those who operated safe havens had to be very secretive. Thus, it is difficult to research the stations on the Underground Railroad. Sadly, escape did not mean permanent freedom—bounty hunters roamed the countryside looking for those who had fled.

Militia companies were being formed across the land. In Frederick, the local fire companies also gathered for military drill.

TO THE PEOPLE OF FRED'K. COUNTY.

FELLOW-CITIZENS,

The wide-spread prevalence of the political heresy of Secession which has resulted in the withdrawal of seven States from that Union which for nearly a century has been our pride and boast, demands our instant action, so that our silence may not be misconstrued and that our example may afford moral aid and encouragement to the loyal & patriotic men who still cling to their Country with unabated love and fidelity.

Notwithstanding the many grievances of which the South justly complains, and against which none has juster cause for remonstrance than the State of Maryland, yet Secession is no remedy for these evils, but on the contrary, is an intolerable aggravation of and an addition to them.

We hold that in a government of laws, the first duty of every citizen is obedience. That whatever injustice or wrong may be perpetrated, in a free government where the largest exercise of liberty compatible with the stability of government and the security of the people is guaranteed to every individual, no such wrong or injustice can be permanent, but that a fair and candid appeal to the honesty and intelligence of the people of the whole country, will inevitably result in a full and cordial recognition of all our constitutional rights and the removal of all our existing grounds of complaint.

We hold that the temporary and accidental triumph of the Republican Party in the election of a President, while the real and substantial triumph of the government remained in the hands of their opponents, was no such screw-to-having calamity as to compel or justify the dissolution of the Confederacy; the total abandonment of our rights and privilege in the Union and the renunciation of the glorious heritage bequeathed to us by our Revolutionary ancestors.

In returning sense of justice on the part of our Northern brethren, and we feel justified in believing that there is already a past or personal cause, to unite with them in

Therefore, the undersigned earnestly invite their fellow-citizens of Frederick County, who stand by the Union of these States and oppose Secession for any

MASS CONVENTION

AT THE COURT HOUSE, IN THE CITY OF FREDERICK AT 10 O'CLOCK,

ON TUESDAY, THE 26TH DAY OF MARCH, 1861

to form a Union Organization in this County and to take steps for holding a Union State Convention at an early day thereafter,

Jacob Bear, R. Potts, L. J. Brengle, John Louis, Chas E Trail, Wm P Mansby, James Cooper, Frederick Schley, Grayson Eichelberger, James Whitehill, Edward Shriver, Adam Wolfe, Nicholas Whittmore, Wm D Reese, J W L Carty, Basil Norris, W Tyler, Sr, Jacob Markell, H T Stokes, John Schreiner, R H Margill, P L Storm, W B Tyler, Francis Markell, P M Englebrecht, George Markell, Lewis Markell, Emanuel Mantz, John Ramsburgh, Jacob Knauff, George A. Abbott, John McPherson, Saml. R. Preston, Dewalt Willard, Samuel Cormack, J. McPhercon, Nelsons Ramsburg, Jacob Grove, Jacob Reich, John J Green, Hiram Schmeder, Philip Cramer

Otho Norris, J D Getzendanner, Ulysses Hobbs, Charles Cole, J A Simmons, Frederick Keefer, Christian Steiner, Charles Lease, James T Smith, D C Winebrenner, James Hopwood, Barney Fisher, James Hergesheimer, Zephaniah Harrison, J Gault, Edward Buckey, Thos M Hollbrunner, John Mackechuey, Edward Sinn, Val'n Brunner, Wm G Cole, Tobias Haller, Jacob Himmell, John J Woodward, M Schaeffer, Wm G Schaeffer, M Keefer, T J McGill, George Salmon, Jonathan T. Wilson, William B. James, W. Lechner, W Gittings, Isaac Keller, William T. Preston, W James Simmons, Wm. R. Derr, John H. Gerry, William H Greer, Daniel S. Schoeffer, Charles H Keefer, George W Cramer

Jacob Salum, Jacob Reifsnider, Charles E Mealey, Charles W Haller, Frederick Main, Geo C Johnson, Charles Mantz, E Y Goldsborough, Samuel H Hogg, Jacob Fox, David Weaver, Wm Johnston, Edward Trail, W G Moran, Daniel Haller, George Engelbrecht, Thomas M Markell, William T Haller, John E Siffard, John Goldsborough, George Feyloster, G W Delaplane, Daniel Swcainer, E Albaugh, George W. Ulrich, Abraham Haff, Charles E Albaugh, D T Ronner, Andrew Boyd, Hiram B. Mullen, John H. Abbott, Fairfax Schley, R. G. McPheron, William Stokes, D A Cunningham, John E. Keller, James M. Harding, Henry M. Nixdorff, Henry B Fender, Samuel R. Marsh, Chas E. Campbell, Philip H Sinn

Ephraim Creager, Spencer C Jones, Grafton W Elliott, John Poole, Jacob Detre, William B Boyd, Erasmus Wyst, I S Seibold, G H Kephart, Daniel H Rohr, George K Bircly, D M Brooks, John Lxeth, J W Snmau, C F Albaugh, John T Nebley, Isaiah Mealey, Jacob Sanner, George Negashon, John H Mumford, Robert Boone, David Boyd, Sr, Levi Vanhosern, Dennis Schull, William H. Brish, Jacher Himhory, William Higgins, Richard T. Dixon, Lewis H. Dill, John J. Sunson, Grafton Faut, Anson Unmel, G. W Dretabaugh, W. L Siermesamner, Benjamin Ebert, Jill F Schaafer, A. P Kessler, W G Conard, Henry A Cole

Lewis H. Bennett, P. Jefferson Hawman, Lloyd Dorsey, Robert Shafer, George W. Summers, Henry C. Steiner, John J. Kastner, Laurence Beatz, Daniel A. Staley, Anthony Kimmel, Francis T. Rhodes, George S. Derr, Isaac P. Suman, George W. L. Bartgis, James Wilson, George Gittinger, James Bruner, H. K. Hilton, Michael Engelbrecht, William Glessner, George Kantner, A. H. Hunt, Thos. T. Cromwell, W. R. Sanderson, W. J. Lynn Smith, Suman Parsons, Frederick Shipley, Abraham Kemp, George M. Tyler, Maurice Albaugh, William T. Duvall, Charles W. Eader, George Metzger, Michael H Haller, William Maloney, Benjamin Banezabad, George H Miller, Christian Worrner, Henry A Cole

Daniel S. Loy, William Dean, W. H. C. Dean, Josiah Harman, Harrison Conley, Nicholas T. Haller, L M Englebrecht, James W. Phelon, I Getzendanner, John T. Martin, Henry Lorentz, William Lorentz, John Routzabu, Mathias Ahalt, John Sifford, Geo T. Willard, Thomas Hooper, John Cramer, James W. Itom, J George Sinn, J. R. Markoto, John Hooper, William Hooper, James Hooper, W. H. R. Kelly, O. F. Butler, Gideon Bantz, David Kenoga, Upton Buhrman, W. L. Hays, A. E. Smith, Clark Kildredge, H. G. Arnold, Hamos T. C. Green, J. J. Micea, George B. Drouis, Dr. J. Boone, J. A. Brengle, Jr, G. J. Dull, Jacob Wong, T. M. Morgan, jr

Printed at the Office of "The Maryland Union," Frederick, Md. [March 19, 1861.]

The proclamation to Frederick County. *Frederick County Archives.*

Dr. William Nelson Pendleton had departed Frederick in 1854 to assume the pastorate of an Episcopal church in Lexington, Virginia. There, being a West Point graduate, he trained the famed Rockbridge Artillery. In 1856, a new political party was formed in Wisconsin. With an antislavery platform, the members chose their first candidates: the pathfinder John C. Fremont for president.

Events do not happen in a vacuum. Often something happening far away has a profound effect on local persons or places. Such were some of the events preceding and taking place during the Civil War. Because of these events and circumstances, places like Frederick, Antietam and Gettysburg become part of the story. Political decisions, the abolitionist movement and the *Dred Scott* decision led to Frederick becoming the crossroads of the war.

Another event was about to take place some twenty miles west of Frederick. One man's actions agitated the people in the South and brought war a step closer. He had caused a lot of trouble in Kansas, and now he had come to Washington County. His name was John Brown.

On July 4, 1859, John Unseld rode from the farm he owned near Dargan. He was retired now, and others did his work for him. He was going to Harpers Ferry for a big holiday drink. Soon he met a bearded man by the name of Isaac Smith, who introduced his two sons and a man by the name of Anderson.

Unseld, like most people of the area, knew everybody else. He soon recognized that these men were strangers. He asked them if they were going to stay. Isaac Smith replied that it all depended on the cost of land.

Unseld, trying to be helpful, said:

> *Up the road toward Sharpsburg is old Doc Kennedy's place. He died a short time ago, and his widow'd like to sell or rent. It's not very big, thirty acres or so, but it'd do until you get settled here. The big house with two stories is on our right, and then there's a little cabin on the left.*[2]

Ambrose Burnside. *Library of Congress.*

Unseld had no idea that he had been talking not to Isaac Smith but to John Brown. The four newcomers walked from Sandy Hook to the farm and decided that it was adequate for their plans. The kitchen was in the basement, living room and bedrooms were on the second floor and an attic hid things they wanted to keep out of sight.

During the summer of 1859, Brown soon gathered twenty-one men to the Kennedy farm. He paid thirty-five dollars to ensure the rent. He sent to North Elba, New York, requesting his sixteen-year-old daughter, Annie, to come and keep house for the men. Oliver Brown's seventeen-year-old wife, Martha, was to come along, too.

Folks in Sharpsburg and neighbors soon became curious about the wagons containing long boxes seen heading to the Kennedy farm. "Isaac Smith" said, "Oh, that's just our prospecting machinery." But in reality, the boxes contained Sharps rifles and pikes to arm the slaves and overthrow the government.

Annie Brown said that "after breakfast Father usually read a chapter in the Bible and made a plain, short, sensible prayer, standing while praying."[3] Then Annie cleared the table and swept the floor. She also had another assignment, watching for Mrs. Huffmaster, the nearest neighbor. She was like a flea, constantly around. Thus Annie had to sound the alarm so that the men could hide. Clothing was often washed at night and hung out in the darkness, thereby preventing nosy neighbors from seeing the many shirts and trousers.

Annie said, "I was there to keep the outside world from discovering that John Brown and his men were in the neighborhood."[4]

On Sunday, October 16, 1859, John Brown read his Bible and had devotions with his little army. A light mist was falling, and at 8:00 p.m. he announced, "Come on boys. Get your arms. We're going to the Ferry." The hour had come. Brown was ready to strike—and the rest is history.[5]

At 10:30 p.m., Brown seized the Baltimore & Ohio Railroad over the Potomac River. Shortly thereafter, the Raiders occupied the U.S. Arsenal and Armory. Brown proceeded to cut telegraph wires and sent raiding parties into the countryside to gather hostages. One of the places was the home of a relative of George Washington. An eastbound train soon arrived; however, the engineer had learned of the troubles and refused to cross until daylight. For some unexplained reason, Brown permitted the train to proceed. Arriving at Monocacy Junction, the engineer related the news of what was occurring at Harpers Ferry. Shooting also erupted at the ferry. A freed African American by the name of Hayward Shepherd, who was the station master, was the first unfortunate person to be killed, ironically.

As October 17 dawned, the fire alarm bells in Frederick began to ring. The local firemen militia hurried to their engine house and thence to Monocacy Junction. There they boarded a train headed for Harpers Ferry. Colonel Robert E. Lee, and a young lieutenant by the name of James Ewell Brown "Jeb" Stuart, plus a detachment of marines arrived later.

When marines and the Frederick militia arrived at Harpers Ferry, they were joined by other Virginia militia from Charles Town and Shepherdstown. When darkness fell, Brown, his raiders and the hostages gathered in the fire engine house at the armory. The next morning, after refusing to surrender, the marines stormed the engine house, battered down the door and captured Brown and the raiding party.

Many in the North welcomed the news of Brown's raid. It was a different story in the South. The Southern states looked on his act as treason and an attack on their way of life. Rallies were held in the North and South. Fiery speeches were given both for and against Brown's act. Some Southern cadets at West Point considered leaving the academy.

A week after the raid, Brown was brought to trial in Charles Town, Virginia (now West Virginia). He was indicted for treason against Virginia and for "conspiring with the slaves to commit treason and murder." Brown refused to offer a plea of insanity. Again, he looked upon himself as a prophet and a man sent to deliver the African Americans.

On December 2, 1859, throngs crowded Charles Town. Included in the gathering was a stern, blue-eyed major from the Virginia Military Institute. His name was Thomas J. Jackson. He was in command of a contingent of cadets. They had been ordered to Charles Town to support the local militia. No one knew quite what to expect.

The crowd, militia and cadets were on hand for the hanging of the abolitionist John Brown. As Brown went to the gallows, he made a chilling prediction. "I, John Brown am now quite certain that the crimes of this guilty land can never be purged away but with blood. I had, as I now think, vainly flattered myself that without very much bloodshed, it might be done."[6]

The nation was drifting toward war. There was much division in the land, and the Buchanan administration seemed powerless to halt the drift.

With Brown's death, the North and abolitionists had a martyr, while the South saw evil clouds on the horizon. Sectionalism and the issues of slavery and states' rights had reached a point of no return. Heated passions made it difficult for moderates to debate and seek a peaceful solution.

While the Republican Party was antislavery, there was deep division within the ranks of the Democrats. The leading candidate was Stephen A. Douglas, a senator from Illinois, and a party to the famed Lincoln-Douglas debates. He embraced "the Freeport Doctrine." Many from the South felt that the issue should be decided by a congressional vote. They feared more events similar to the John Brown raid and stressed the rights of the states to decide matters.

On April 23, 1860, the Democratic Convention met in Charleston, South Carolina. Immediately there was bitter wrangling. Western and Northern delegates strongly supported Douglas, while the westerners felt that each new state should decided the question of slavery, not the U.S. Congress. This infuriated Southern delegates. They were faced with accepting Douglas's idea of popular or state sovereignty. The Douglas platform was adopted, and the Southerners walked out—Douglas and his platform was as bad as the Republican approach.

Some others met in Richmond and decided to wait and see what happened at the upcoming Republican Convention. Some older politicians did not wait. They met in Baltimore and formed "the Constitutional Party," naming as their candidates John Bell and Edward Everett. They called for the strict support of the Constitution and the union of states.

The Democrats reconvened in Baltimore. The session was slow in getting started. Three days were spent arguing over credentials. When some delegates from Alabama and Louisiana were admitted, anti-Douglas delegates walked out. The seeds of anger and discontent were growing larger by the day. The debates and contention are stories in themselves. Douglas was finally accepted as the primary candidate. However, there would soon be a third Democratic candidate: John Breckinridge, vice president in the Buchanan administration, was selected by the proslavery delegates. Many thought that every vote for him would be a vote for

Southern independence. Now the Democrats had three candidates—and a divided electorate.

On November 6, 1860, the American people cast their ballots. Stephen A. Douglas, in his bid for the presidency, received 1,376,957 votes, along with just 12 electoral votes. Bell and Edward Everett, the Constitutional Party candidates, received nearly 600,000 votes and 39 electoral votes. Breckinridge and Lane, the candidates of the Southern Democrats, acquired 849,781 votes, along with 72 electoral votes. Abraham Lincoln, the Rail-Splitter, received 1,866,542 votes along with 180 votes in the electoral column. Thus, Lincoln was elected.

In Maryland, Douglas received twice as many votes as Lincoln, who received but 2,294 votes. Balloting in Frederick County reflected the widespread national division. Douglas and those strongly in favor of the Union received 3,609 votes. Breckinridge and the newly formed group favoring slavery and states' rights acquired 3,617 votes, and Abraham Lincoln, the "Black Republican," got but 103 votes. In the voting districts of Urbana, Mount Pleasant and Petersville, Mr. Lincoln did not receive a single vote.

In December 1860, a large group of Fredericktonians gathered and formulated a resolution:

> *We believe and are firmly convinced that to secure peace to our beloved country there should be speedily inaugurated in the Northern States of our Confederacy such conciliatory measures as would quiet the present apprehensions of our Southern brethren and secure confidence in the recognition of their rights for the future, and that such a course would strengthen our Federal Union which was planned by the wisdom and cemented with the blood of pure and patriotic men who have gone before us.*

Meanwhile, to the south, another meeting had occurred. It had far-reaching consequences and soon affected Frederick more than the local decision. William Henry Gist, the Charleston firebrand, was instrumental in having the governor of the Palmetto State call a meeting to act on Southern rights and secession. Something needed to be done for the "manliness of the South."

The people of Charleston gathered in the streets, awaiting the verdict. Flags and bunting hung from balconies and porches. Torchlights blazed.

It was almost like a gala celebration on New Year's Eve. Then, at last, the throng learned of the news:

> *We the People of the State of South Carolina, in Convention assembled do declare and ordain, and it is hereby declared and ordained.*
>
> *That the Ordinance adopted by us in Convention, on the twenty-third day of May, in the year of our Lord one thousand seven hundred and eighty-eight, whereby the Constitution of the United States of America was ratified, and also all acts of the General Assembly of this State, ratifying amendments of the said Constitution, are hereby repealed; and that union now subsisting between South Carolina and other States, under the name of "The United States of America," is hereby dissolved.*

That evening, in the presence of a great crowd, every member of the convention signed the ordinance. When the last signature was completed, the audience broke into a storm of applause and cheers. Outside and inside the hall, the city went wild with excitement. Bells were rung and cannons fired salutes. People shouted and hugged one another. The people of South Carolina had spoken and acted.

But the cards were stacked against the South. The 1860 census showed 31 million Americans. Of these, 22 million lived in the North or in states remaining loyal to the Union. The South could claim only one city of 100,000 population or more, the city of New Orleans. The North had nearly twenty thousand miles of railroads compared to about ten thousand in the South.

The people of the North were shocked by South Carolina's act. They thought that the move would be short-lived. But in January 1861, Mississippi, Florida, Alabama, Georgia and Louisiana—and Texas in February—followed in the steps of South Carolina.

On February 4, delegates from these states met in Montgomery, Alabama, to form a provisional government for the Confederate States of America. On the ninth, Jefferson Davis was chosen as president. A divided nation faced Abraham Lincoln as he prepared to leave his Springfield home.

From the census of 1860, we learn that on the eve of the Civil War, Frederick City had a population of 8,142, with 46,591 listed for the county; 794 owned slaves. There were 2,365 farms. Frederick County was listed as having 665 square miles, with a population density of 70.1. According to the census, there were 21,128 horses in the county, with 21,400 cattle and 10,389 sheep. To feed the family and livestock, the county produced almost one million bushels of wheat and slightly more than one million bushels of corn. Frederick County ranked number one in the state in the production of wheat and corn. The worth of real estate was listed as $16,290,000. The worth of the average family was $3,603.75.

Chapter 3

SPARKS AND FIRE, 1861

On March 4, 1861, Abraham Lincoln was inaugurated as the sixteenth president of the United States. Standing with Lincoln, and administering the oath of office, was Chief Justice Roger Brooke Taney. Lincoln had a task before him greater than the one that faced George Washington. The unfinished dome of the Capitol was symbolic of the unfinished work before Lincoln. Some even wondered whether the situation could be resolved. In his address to the gathered throng, Lincoln was conciliatory: "We are not enemies, but friends...through passion may be strained, it must not break our bonds of affection...in your hands, my dissatisfied fellow countrymen, not in mine, is the momentous issue of Civil War."

As the Southern states withdrew from the Union, they seized virtually all federal property within their boundaries. On March 5, Lincoln received bad news. Major Robert Anderson, commanding the Union garrison in Charleston Harbor, sent word that his command was running low on supplies. He felt there would be difficulty in resupplying unless the Union showed force. He thought that the South Carolina militia would deny any attempt to bring provisions to the garrison.

Lincoln was in a quandary. To back down and withdraw from the garrison would show weakness and acceptance of Southern demands, while a show of force might precipitate armed conflict. Lincoln, therefore, dispatched his friend Ward Hill Lamon to speak with the governor of South Carolina. However, at this point, talk was useless. With the odds against him, Lincoln decided to send supplies to Fort Sumter. He notified South Carolina authorities of his intention.

Francis Pickens, the governor of South Carolina, met with his cabinet and ordered General P.G.T. Beauregard, in command of Charleston Harbor, to demand that the federal garrison at Fort Sumter evacuate. If not, South Carolina would take it by force. On April 11, Beauregard demanded the surrender of the fort. Anderson refused to comply.

Then, on April 12 at 4:30 a.m., sparks lighted fuses and the first shots of the war were fired as Confederate batteries began their bombardment of Fort Sumter. Seeing that defense was useless, Anderson surrendered. Jubilation reigned in the South.

Lincoln then called for seventy-five thousand troops to put down the rebellion. This prompted North Carolina, Tennessee and Arkansas to join the ranks of the Confederacy. And the call for troops pushed Virginia and Robert E. Lee over the brink. The Civil War (or the War of the Rebellion or the War Between the States) was on. And the sparks ignited at Fort Sumter would see Frederick become the crossroads of the war.

As Lincoln was calling for troops to put down the rebellion, the legislature, fearing problems in Maryland, called upon the governor to have all militia units return their weapons and other equipment to the armories. This angered the militia units. They were not about to give up their weapons. The Frederick home guards stated that they would "[r]esist the enforcement of this order at all hazards and unto death." Fearing more trouble, the state government rescinded the order.

While Frederick and western Maryland tended to be more conservative and more sympathetic to the Union, Baltimore and the Eastern Shore had Southern leanings and believed strongly in states' rights.

Thus it was no surprise that serious problems erupted in Baltimore. On April 5, President Lincoln called for seventy-five thousand volunteers to serve for three months to put down the insurrection. On April 18, four companies of the Twenty-fifth Pennsylvania departed from Harrisburg en route to Washington. When they arrived at Bolton Station in Baltimore, they were surrounded by a hostile "hooting, yelling crowd." They were also pelted with bricks and stones. One member of the unit suffered a severe head wound.

More trouble was on the horizon. The various tracks in Baltimore had different gauges. Therefore, soldiers had to disembark at one station and march to another to continue the journey to Washington. Sometimes cars were uncoupled and then pulled by horses to the next station. On April 19, the famed, or infamous, Baltimore Riot occurred.

When the Sixth Massachusetts Volunteers reached Philadelphia, the commander, Colonel Edward Jones, received word that Southern forces were awaiting them in Baltimore. He ordered every soldier to load his weapon. Sure enough, debris had been piled on the tracks in Baltimore. However, instead of Southern troops, it was an angry mob that awaited the lads from Massachusetts.

Upon their arrival, the regiment was pelted with rocks, bottles and virtually any object that could be thrown. Some of the soldiers were wounded, and shots rang out. At this point, the soldiers fired a volley killing or wounding several citizens. Mayor of Baltimore George W. Brown tried in vain to stop the melee. Chaos reigned supreme. When it was over, several soldiers were numbered among the slain, with another thirty-six wounded. Twelve citizens were killed and many others wounded. The residents of Baltimore were enraged. They felt that they had been victimized. Maryland was very close to secession. Papers in the North labeled Baltimore as a "hotbed of secession." Maryland governor Hicks and Mayor Brown sent a message to President Lincoln asking for assistance in keeping the law. Maryland militia was also ordered to Baltimore. Rumors were afloat that Southern sympathizers were ready to attack Fort McHenry. For the next few weeks, Baltimore was an armed camp. Some think that had Governor Hicks or Mayor Brown taken the lead, Maryland would have expanded the cause of secession. Acting on his own, Benjamin Butler, later nicknamed "the Beast," occupied Annapolis and Baltimore.

The event had far-reaching consequences. James Ryder Randall, a Marylander teaching in Louisiana, read an account of the explosion in Baltimore. That night, he composed a nine-stanza poem called "My Maryland." Jennie and Hettie Cary, sisters living in Baltimore, changed the title to "Maryland, My Maryland." It became a favorite of Confederate soldiers, and in 1939," Maryland, My Maryland" became the official state song. In recent years, it has become controversial, as it speaks, among other things, about "the despot's heal is on thy shores." The reader is referred to Daniel Carroll's fine book, *The Civil War in Maryland*.

Fearing Union reprisals for the troubles in Baltimore, a call was sent for Maryland militia units to hasten to Baltimore. In the vanguard were Captain Bradley Johnson and the Frederick Mounted Guards. The men armed themselves with double-barreled shotguns and buckshot. They would be efficient at close range. The men remained in Baltimore until April 25.

The Baltimore Riots, or Baltimore Massacre, led in part to other events. Governor Thomas Hicks called for a special session of the Maryland legislature. He had delayed in calling a session because he felt that the tide would swing to the South that the legislators might pass an ordinance of secession or in some manner support the Confederacy.

Annapolis being occupied by General Butler, and not wishing to offend pro-Southerners in the legislature, Hicks called for a special session to convene in Frederick on April 26, 1861 at 1:00 p.m. In his communiqué, Governor Hicks tried to avoid showing favoritism to the defense of the Union or recognition of the newly formed Confederate States of America.

A memorial from Prince George's County requested immediate passage of an act of secession. The legislature met in Frederick from April 26 to May 14.

A letter was sent to the governor of Virginia stating the concerns of the state of Maryland. This brought an immediate reply, stating that "if at any time the military forces of Virginia trespassed or temporarily occupied the soil of Maryland, with…no hostile intent, any and all damages to persons and property would be reimbursed."

The response from Maryland was: "Be it resolved by the General Assembly of Maryland that Maryland will rely upon the honor of Virginia for full recompense for all property destroyed by said troops."

The "extra session" was begun on Friday, April 26. The initial meeting was held at the Frederick County Courthouse and then shifted to Kemp Hall, a building owned by the German Reformed Church at the corner of North Market Street and Church Street.

A bill was presented by Baltimore asking for $45,000 for the defense of that city. The division existing in the state is seen in the fact that it was not until June 7 that the Senate delegates approved the flying of the national flag on Kemp Hall. The House did not approve it until June 31.

On June 20, Federal troops began rounding up and imprisoning some of the members of the Maryland House and Senate. Ross Winans, a delegate from Baltimore, was actually arrested in the presence of Governor Hicks. Winans was imprisoned in Annapolis and then at Fort McHenry by an executive order of President Lincoln. By a vote of forty-one to eight, the House and Senate then passed a resolution of protest to be sent to the president.

In the resolution, they said that they recognized the federal situation but were doing all they could to remedy the problems in Maryland. They condemned the president and the federal government for stating "that the said act of the President of the United States and declare the thing to be a gross usurpation, unjust, oppressive, tyrannical, and an utter violation of the common right and of the plain provision of the Constitution."

Recognizing the geographical and transportation importance of Frederick, Union troops arrived to secure the city. The regiment was the First Rhode Island Volunteers, commanded by then colonel Ambrose Burnside. He was a West Point graduate and close friend of George B. McClellan. He had also invented a carbine. Burnside later commanded the forces occupying Annapolis and led a successful expedition to capture Southern forts along the Carolina coast. Initially, Burnside and his 1,100-men command were sent to Williamsport, Maryland, located on the north shore of the Potomac. Patrols also operated in Greencastle and Hagerstown.

Burnside later issued a letter of thanks to the communities that had kindly received his troops. He noted: "Particular thanks are due to the citizens of Frederick City, Maryland, for the hearty welcome they extended and the lavish hospitality they dispensed to the regiment. Their good will is fully reciprocated and their kindness will long be remembered."

A major incident during this time occurred when the editor of the *Frederick Herald* raised a Southern flag. A group of citizens and soldiers threatened to burn the building. Burnside arrived on the scene and restored order by ordering the flag to be removed and the crowd to disperse.

The division and bitter feelings remained. Some were arrested by Union troops for their written and vocal remarks. John W. Baughman, the editor of the *Frederick Citizen*, was among them. He had written strongly against the United States and the Lincoln administration.

Many persons thought that the war would be of short duration. In the beginning, both the North and the South were alive with patriotic fervor, speeches and parades. Ladies in various towns and cities took their finest material and made battle flags for the various companies and regiments. Of course, the soldiers vowed never to "disgrace the flag and to carry it triumphantly to victory over the foes."

Meanwhile, politicians were clamoring for action. Raw militia came together. They had little knowledge of military fundamentals. Many officers were elected to command by popular vote and had little more knowledge than the average man in the ranks. Even West Point graduates had little experience of commanding large bodies of men.

On Sunday, July 21, 1861, Major General Irvin McDowell led Union troops into battle against Confederates commanded by Pierre G.T. Beauregard. The Confederates were in place along a sluggish Virginia stream by the name of Bull Run near Manassas Junction. Early in the action, the North seemed to be on the verge of victory. Then a Confederate brigade made a defiant stand on a hill near the home of Judith Henry. General Bee shouted, "There stands Jackson like a stone wall! Rally behind the Virginians!" The tide turned, and the battle became a Union rout. Then the realization of war set in, and the North and South prepared for an indefinite state of strife.

Meanwhile, the federal government and the State of Maryland continued to spar over the problem of loyalty to the Union versus secession. The die was cast. September 17 was ironically the anniversary of the signing of the Constitution and, a year later, the Battle of Antietam. The local newspaper carried the story:

LEGISLATORS ARRESTED
NINE APPREHENDED
IN FREDERICK CITY
PICKETS SURROUND CITY
CLERK CALLS ROLL TO EMPTY CHAMBER
Brewer Refuses Oath
Naill, Fiery Refuse To Attend Session
Heavy Guard Assigned To Prisoners On Train
Ends Special Session
CITY CONTROL RESTORED TO CIVIL AUTHORITIES

FREDERICK, MD., Sept. 18—Nine members of the Maryland Legislature were arrested here yesterday and today and taken to Annapolis, by order of Maj. Gen. Nathaniel P. Banks, commander of the U.S. Department of the Shenandoah.

The Legislature was to meet in special session in the German Reformed building in this city yesterday. Banks received orders from Simon Cameron, Secretary of War, on Sept. 11 in which the latter stated: "The passage of any act of secession by the legislature of Maryland must be prevented. Exercise your own judgment as to the time and manner, but do the work effectively."

Yesterday at 1 p.m., when the Legislature was to assemble, only three Senators were in town. S.J. Bradley of Queen Anne's County, Anthony Kimmell of Frederick County and Tilghrnan Nuttle of Caroline County. They refused to enter the Senate Chamber but met for consultation in the Reading Room across the hall. They informed the clerk that they proposed to consult as to their course and would communicate their joint determination in a half hour.

Clerk Calls Roll

William Kilgour, Clerk of the Senate, went through the formality of calling the roll to the empty chamber and announced that "there being no quorum present, the Senate stands adjourned until one o'clock tomorrow." At 1:30 p.m., notice was given to the three senators of the clerk's action.

Shortly after both houses adjourned, a cordon of armed pickets moved into and surrounded this city with instructions to allow no one to pass without a written permit from a member of Gen. Banks's staff, who had been appointed provost marshal. A squad of police officers from Baltimore accompanied by troops of the Third Wisconsin Regiment, commanded by Col. T.H. Ruger, commenced to search the city for the parties they were ordered to arrest.

E. Riley, editor of the Annapolis Republican and printer of the House, was taken into custody. Several citizens of this city were arrested for using disloyal language; they were William Mason, John Hagan, John W. Elkin, Edward A. Hanson and William Hanson and his two sons.

Rose Hill Manor. *Author's collection.*

*The afternoon train which usually leaves here at 1 p.m. was detained
until 3 p.m. today to take the prisoners to Annapolis. The delay was
occasioned to give some of the prisoners an opportunity to obtain their
discharge by taking the oath of allegiance. The oath was given to the
following, which were then released: E. Riley, Milton Y. Kidd, Thomas
H. Moore, William Kilgour, S.P. Carmack and the citizens of this
city who were arrested yesterday. John H. Brewer, reading clerk of the
Senate, refused to take the oath and was dispatched in the cars with the
nine arrested members of the House.* [1]

With Frederick being at the crossroads, the city and surrounding
area had to be secured. Thus, Nathaniel Banks and his command were
ordered to occupy the city.

At the outbreak of the Civil War, the regular United States Army was
very small. Many of the officers, West Point graduates, went with the
South. Initially looking on the war as a lark, wealthy businessmen raised
and equipped companies and even regiments. They felt that this entitled
them to the rank of colonel, even though they did not know the first thing
about the military. In other situations, officers were elected by popular vote.
Then there were the political generals. Such a man was Nathaniel Banks.

Born in 1816, Banks had served in Congress during the years 1853–57. The next three years were spent in the governor's office. He was also president of the Illinois Central Railroad. Having friends in high places and using his political clout, Banks, on May 16, 1861, was appointed major general of Massachusetts Volunteers.

One of the persons with the Nathaniel Banks's army was Alpheus S. Williams, commanding a brigade of infantry. Williams was born on September 20, 1810, in the state of Connecticut. His parents died when he was young, but he received a substantial sum of money in his mother's will. He graduated from Yale University in 1831 and traveled at home and abroad. In 1836, Williams arrived in Detroit and made the city his home. He married a young widow by the name of Jane Herford on January 16, 1839. Sadly, Mrs. Williams died at the age of thirty.

Williams was a man of great energy. He became a prominent lawyer and president of a bank and published a newspaper; he then became postmaster for the city of Detroit. Being interested in the military, Williams became a member of Detroit's Brady Guards. He served in the Mexican-American War as a brigadier of the Michigan Volunteers. At the outbreak of the Civil War, Williams was sent to Fort Wayne to train troops. Then he was ordered to Washington and became a brigade commander under Banks.

When Williams departed for the East, his son Charles and daughters Mary and Irene, both teenagers, remained in Detroit. The general wrote to them faithfully. From his letters, we gain descriptions of life and activity in Frederick. Wearing a long beard and being in his forties, Williams was affectionately called "Old Pap" by his troops.[2]

Early December found Williams heading for Frederick. It was lovely Indian summer weather. The command reached Monocacy Junction without wagons and had to bivouac minus tents. The night was rather frosty. Williams found shelter in a nice farmhouse near Urbana. He had a room all to himself, the first in two months. Additionally, there was a pretty woman. He noted that he had not seen "a passable face for a long time."

The next day, Williams and his brigade marched through Frederick with their colors flying. They entered in grand style, with the band playing. His troops were complimented, the people saying that they made the best appearance yet. Williams said, "I rode at the head of my Brigade with my staff of six. The whole population was out and the flag of our Union displayed very generously."[3]

December 7, 1861, found Williams perched on the chain of hills about three and a half miles west of Frederick. Headquarters of the brigade was located in a farmer's house. He noted:

> *The country about us is exceedingly beautiful: and picturesque between the Catoctin and South Mountain lies the most beautiful and fertile valley* [the Middletown Valley].
>
> *To the East is the ancient and rather fine looking city, a place of several thousand inhabitants…at a distance, its lofty spires…and public edifices give it a very picturesque appearance.*[4]

Williams told his daughter to address communications to "Headquarters, 3rd Brigade, Gen. Banks, Division near Frederick." He also noted that the weather had been charming and that his brigade had participated in several reviews. Local residents often visited the campsites. Thanksgiving was held under a canvas tent, but they had turkey and chicken.

Some snow and sleet fell on December 23, and it was also a blue day as a Union soldier was executed for shooting his commander. The general noted that Wednesday would be Christmas Day. "Never before have we been absent from one another at Christmas…while you can remember the happy scenes of the past, but you can look joyfully to the future."

Wilder Dwight was a native of Springfield, Massachusetts. He loved good books and by an early age had a fine library. Graduating from Harvard, he became a lawyer. When the war broke out, Dwight helped organize the Second Massachusetts Infantry. The unit was sometimes called the Harvard Regiment as sixteen of its officers were Harvard graduates. Their names are inscribed on a memorial arch at the university.

The Second Massachusetts made camp on the east bank of the Monocacy, beyond the old Jug Bridge. Young officer Dwight wrote: "Frederick is a fine old town." The regimental band leader was already planning to give concerts in the city. "The principal duty will be keeping the men in order, and preventing drunkenness." The bivouac was named Camp Hicks, after the wartime governor of Massachusetts.

On December 9, Dwight rode into Frederick:

As I came over the hill which slopes down to the Monocacy Bridge and overlooks the city and Valley of Frederick, I could not but enjoy the scene. There lay the city with its spires and buildings clear in the sunlight...Peace and plenty were in the landscape.[5]

Some ladies of the town asked Major Dwight for the protection of their homes. And some of the local people advised keeping quiet on the slavery issue, "wait and see how it will be resolved." By December 11, Dwight, expecting to be at Camp Hicks for the winter, began building a house, nine feet square. This was located between four trees, with a wood floor and the tent over the boards. The furniture consisted of a bed, washstand and table. Dwight was also concerned with finding quarters for the one hundred horses that pulled the supply wagons.

The Twenty-seventh Indiana made camp on the farm of Mr. Clay on the road to Ijamsville. There they received their first military pay, gleefully receiving notes and gold coins. "Peddlers as thick as frogs descended on the camp." Some of the men obtained some hard cider. Soon they were very relaxed.[6]

FREDERICK, MD., Dec. 4—Maj. Gen. Nathanial P. Banks arrived at 4 p.m. yesterday and established his headquarters in the house formerly occupied by Bradley T. Johnson in this city.

Banks was accompanied by his staff and body guard. He was escorted to his headquarters on Court Street by the First Regiment of the Potomac Home Brigade, commanded by Col. William P. Maulsby. Bradley T. Johnson is presently absent from this city and is serving in the Confederate army.

Banks' staff consists of Maj. R. Morris Copeland, assistant adjutant general; Capt. D. D. Perkins, Fourth Artillery Inspector and chief of staff; Captains R. S. Shriber, Sheffler and D'Haudeville, aides de camp; Captains Hollibird and Bingham, quartermasters; Capt. Beckwith, commissary; and Surgeon William S. King, medical director.

The headquarters of Banks' and his staff, and the officers of the different brigades are located in this city. The First Brigade, commanded by Brig. Gen. Alpheus S. Williams, is located in the vicinity of Fairview, on the Western Turnpike. The Second Brigade, commanded by Brig. Gen. John J. Abercrombie, is stationed southeast of this city, on the Monocacy River, near the Baltimore Turnpike Bridge. The Third Brigade, commanded by Brig. Gen. Charles S. Hamilton, is stationed about one mile south of the First Brigade, between the Baltimore Turnpike and the Baltimore and Ohio Railroad.

It is reported that Mrs. Banks will join Gen. Banks here. The members of Banks' staff are quartered in other residences throughout the city. Of the new influx of soldiers, one editor has reported:

"Our usually quiet inland city is now all life and bustle; business is brisk, throngs of soldiers and citizens crowd the streets incessantly, while the passing to and from of detachments of troops, enlivened with the notes of the drum and fife, the inspiriting bugle and music from military bands, the brilliant and varied military costumes and the rush of ladies attracted by the gay scene and tempted forth by the balmy atmosphere, conspire to give a strange and exciting aspect to the town and it is difficult in the din and apparent confusion to recognize its identity."

Union troops arrive in Frederick. *Frederick County Archives.*

Wilder Dwight. *Massachusetts State Archives.*

Reviews occurred frequently in December. Edmund Brown of the Twenty-seventh Indiana notes that their unit was reviewed by General Banks one mile north of Frederick on December 12. It is believed that this was at Rose Hill Manor. Wilder Dwight writes of another review on December 15. When it came time to offer the salute, the major's horse reared.

Two of the favorite moments of the day were mail call and the arrival of the newsboy. The chaplain usually distributed the mail. The paperboy announced his arrival by tooting a tin horn. Then the soldiers rolled out of their tents to purchase the paper.

Soldiers have always liked their drinks. The local farmers supplied hard cider, while Wilder Dwight had another problem. A peddler rode into camp with a cart full of nice pies. Hidden in the cart was a barrel of whiskey. Dwight confronted the man and had him drain the barrel. He then warned the nearby farmers and residents of New Market not to do it again.

He notes on December 20 the arrival of a big box of shirts, drawers, handkerchiefs and mittens. Most were gaily colored. The items were distributed among the men. They did not worry about the proper size or how they fit. For a moment, the soldiers were like children. The regiment also received a supply of new white gloves that made them look very good on parade.

Sadly, Dwight notes the vacant family circles with young men away at war when Christmas arrives. In 1861, Christmas was not "peace, but a sword." Wilder told the folks at home: "Commemorate the message of the Prince of Peace. Gather the Christmas family circle, and remember the absent for family ties are never so close as in those days of separation and trial. Love to all at home."[7]

On the twenty-third. Dwight writes: "Our wooded camp has been hail rattled and rain rattled all night." The trees were crowned with ice, and the gray dawn brought snow. Letters and gifts from home brightened his day. On Christmas Day, Wilder stuck his head out of his tent as the bugler sounded reveille. The moon was still high in the sky. "A light fall of snow, sent by Heaven to gladden the day, had whitened tent and ground alike." The band played "Auld Lang Syne" as Dwight's thoughts turned to home and family, as no doubt did the thoughts of many men camped on "the banks of the Monocacy."[8]

On January 5, General Banks was in church when an officer called him from the service. Jackson was threatening Hancock, Maryland, and the nearby railroad bridges. The men were ordered to gather two days' rations and be ready to march. General Williams and the Third Brigade were sent in the snow from Williamsport toward Hancock. But Jackson was gone, headed for Romney.

There were the lighter moments for the troops, especially the officers. A grand concert was held in Frederick. Full dress uniforms were required. "The hall was crowded. All the beauty and fashion of Frederick were there. The band closed the evening with 'Hail Columbia,' and 'The Star Spangled Banner.'"[9]

January 17 began four days of bone-chilling cold, snow and sleet. Then, a few days later, mud was everywhere, "deep, miry, insidious mud." On the nineteenth, Dwight wished that he had the "wings of the morning" so he could take them to the family home in Brookline. However, he had to content himself with "a web footed, amphibious existence in the mud of Maryland." He had grown to like the tune, but not the words, of "Maryland, My Maryland."

On February 25, the lads from Massachusetts were ready to break camp and move out for the spring campaign. In the rain and fog, "we splashed and paddled to Frederick." At the depot, the band played "The Girl I Left Behind Me." And the girls of Frederick wept. Then the train left for Monocacy Junction, Sandy Hook and Harpers Ferry.

Nathaniel Banks's troops were being sent to Winchester to oppose a Confederate force led by Thomas J. "Stonewall" Jackson. Dwight would be back in Frederick in the autumn of 1862, on his way to action and death in the cornfield at Antietam.

For more information, see the Jacob Engelbrecht Diaries, Frederick County Archives, as well as the issues of the Frederick Examiner *and the commemorative program of the centennial meeting of the Maryland legislature.*

Chapter 4

"Up from the Meadows Rich with Corn"

The creaking of wheels, the smells of sweaty leather harnesses, the rumble of wagons, the *tramp-tramp* of marching men, the clouds of dust—and the great thirst. This was September 1862. Armies were on the march, headed for Fredericktown, the crossroads of history, and eventually a battle that turned the tide of history at Antietam Creek, twenty-five miles west of Frederick.

Although troops had been in Frederick, the city had been spared armed conflict. They had read and heard about the battles at Manassas and in the Shenandoah Valley. Now the citizens of Frederick had a rendezvous with the blue and gray.

At the end of August, Lee and his army had defeated John Pope at Second Manassas. The demoralized Union army fell back to the defenses of Washington. Lee realized that the South could not win a purely defensive war. To remain in Virginia would invite another Yankee move on Richmond.

Thus he wrote to Jefferson Davis proposing a northward movement, crossing the Potomac and entering Maryland. Lee considered his options. Carrying the army westward would put it in the fertile Shenandoah Valley, a terrain with many strategic possibilities, but one in which a retreat would force the army steadily back on the mainline of the Virginia Central Railroad. By elimination, then, destiny beckoned northward across the Potomac. Lee, on September 3, 1862, marched from Chantilly to Leesburg. At the end of the first day's march, Lee wrote to Jefferson Davis, president of the Confederacy:

Robert E. Lee. *Library of Congress.*

The present seems to be the most propitious time since the commencement of the war for the Confederate army to enter Maryland. The two grand armies of the United States that have been operating in Virginia, though now united, are much weakened and demoralized. Their new levies, of which I understand 60,000 men have already been posted in Washington, are not yet organized and will take some time to prepare for the field. If it is ever desired to give material aid to Maryland and afford her an opportunity of throwing off the oppression to which she is now subject, this would seem the most favorable.[1]

These reasons led to the invasion of Maryland:

- *The Union army would be drawn out of Virginia, away from Richmond.*
- *The farmers of Virginia would have the opportunity to harvest their crops, so badly needed to feed the army without Union interference.*

- *A Southern victory on Northern soil would lift the morale of the South and lower that of the North.*
- *A successful invasion might foreshadow final Southern victory if foreign powers came to the aid of the South.*
- *A decisive Confederate victory might cause the North to sue for peace.*
- *It was hoped that many Maryland youth would flock to the Southern cause and help fill the depleted ranks.*
- *Then, too, there was the possibility that an invasion might lead to an uprising, or even cause Maryland to secede, thus surrounding Washington with hostile territory.*[2]

Influenced by these considerations, Lee put the Army of Northern Virginia in motion, and between September 4 and 7 it crossed the Potomac near Leesburg and advanced toward Frederick. Most of the troops crossed via White's Ford, close to the place where the ferry boat *Jubal A. Early* now runs.

The crossing of the Potomac was a holiday for the Marylanders in the Confederate army. All of them were filled with joy, and many wept with gladness when they touched the sacred soil of Maryland. Old and young kissed the sod, and the bands constantly played "Maryland, My Maryland" until the sound became oppressive. The troops were wretchedly clothed and shod. Thousands were without shoes. The wagons were empty except for extra ammunition, and as soon as the troops had crossed, their first meal on Maryland soil were the greens cut from the stalks growing in the cornfields.[3]

The Army of Northern Virginia, about thirty-five thousand strong, pitched their tents just south of Frederick between the Georgetown Road and the Buckeystown Pike with the Monocacy River as the base. Soldiers soon plunged into the river to bathe themselves, as well as their vermin-infested clothing.

Stonewall Jackson was a little stiff and sore. A Marylander sympathetic to the South had given the general a spirited horse. Although he was an excellent rider, the horse had thrown Jackson.

The first weekend in September brought excitement, anticipation and alarm to the area. Morale in the Army of Northern Virginia was very high. They had high hopes that a movement on Baltimore or Harrisburg might bring a Southern victory and independence. Some, basically Union

Thomas J. Jackson. *Library of Congress.*

sympathizers, were filled with anxiety and dread. They did not know what to expect from the Rebels in their midst. On the other hand, those who favored the Southern cause flocked to the bivouac areas, bringing milk and baked goods. They had a good time chatting with the troops.

Robert Moore, a cannoneer in the Rockbridge Artillery, evaded the provost guard and walked into Frederick. His buddy, Steve Dandridge, went along. Moore had a few U.S. dollars. Going to a small store, the two purchased some bread and butter and wine.

Jacob Engelbrecht noted that "by 10 o'clock, the rebels took possession of our good city of Frederick." According to Engelbrecht, "there was no commotion but all was peaceful and quiet. The soldiers were shopping and purchasing shoes, caps, and eatables." He also noted that some of the residents of Frederick had fled northward during the night.[4]

Bradley Johnson, a Fredericktonian and then a colonel in the Confederacy, was quick to "remind the people of the cells of Fort McHenry, the insults to your wives and daughters...the arrests...and midnight searches of your houses."[5] Johnson was named provost marshal, charged with protecting the city from any looting or vandalism.

Sometime during the days of September 6 and 9, a large group of Southern soldiers gathered at the intersection of Market and Patrick Streets and helped themselves to the hats in stock. A photograph captured the event. It remains the only picture of the Confederates in Fredericktown in 1862.[6]

Sunday, September 7, was a gala day in the Confederate camps. Visitors thronged the bivouac area. They were anxious to catch a glimpse of the famed Confederate leaders, especially Lee and Jackson. However, neither Lee nor Jackson were feeling well due to falls. Bouquets of flowers were given to Longstreet and to Jeb Stuart, the Confederate cavalry leader.

During the morning, Jackson was called to Lee's tent. Two young girls who had ridden in a carriage from Baltimore spotted the general and leaped out, running to him. One damsel took his hand. The quiet and shy Jackson was profoundly embarrassed.

After the conference with Lee, Jackson was mobbed again. He spoke briefly with the admiring crowd, but when the admirers sought a lock of his hair, and one from the tail of his horse, he beat a hasty exit and remained secluded until the evening.

Among the visitors were Mrs. Robert Douglas, the mother of Henry Kyd Douglas, and Mrs. Markell. Mrs. Markell brought flowers, and the ladies were graciously received by the Confederate high command.[7]

As the shadows of the day lengthened, the crowd dispersed. However, Thomas Jonathan Jackson had a request. He wanted to go to church. He preferred the Presbyterian church; however, there was no evening service. Ever a stickler for military protocol, he obtained a pass for himself, for Henry Kyd Douglas and for Jackson's brother-in-law, Lieutenant J.G. Morrison. Together they entered the city.

Douglas, being a member of the German Reformed Church and knowing the pastor, Dr. Daniel Zacharias, took the group to the German Reformed Church, now the United Church of Christ on West Church Street.

During the service, Jackson fell asleep. His hand dropped by his side, and his head and chin dropped near his chest. There is no evidence of his snoring. Only the deep tones of the organ awakened him.

Dr. Zacharias was praised for having the courage to pray for President Lincoln in the very presence of "Mighty Stonewall." However, Douglas writes that Jackson never heard the prayer, and if he had, he probably would have said, "Go right ahead and pray for the President, he needs it."[8]

Meanwhile, south of Fredericktown, the reorganized Army of the Potomac, now under the command of George B. McClellan, was at Rockville, about thirty miles away, and ready to move northward.

On Monday, September 8, Brigadier General William Nelson Pendleton rode into Frederick to visit some of his former parishioners. Pendleton was a West Point graduate but then resigned to enter the Episcopal priesthood. From 1846 to 1854, he was the rector of All Saints Episcopal Church on South Court Street. His son, Alexander Swift Pendleton, attended school in Frederick.

While in Frederick, Reverend Pendleton desired to construct a new church. There were good reasons. The congregation was growing, but there was a problem in the summer. There was no air conditioning, and there were several livery stables nearby, too. Naturally the windows had to be opened. The smells and the flies were not conducive to worship. In 1854, Pendleton accepted a call to Lexington, Virginia. There he trained the local militia unit known as the Rockbridge Artillery. He named the cannons "Matthew," "Mark," "Luke" and "John." The cannons are now located at the north edge of the parade ground at the Virginia Military Institute.

Thomas J. Jackson worshiped here on September 17, 1862. *Author's collection.*

Other soldiers also entered Frederick. They knew that the army would soon be on the move. They wanted to purchase an army staple: coffee. Some became angry when storekeepers raised the prices on them, but they caused no trouble.

Lee's plan was to wait at Frederick until he received some favorable responses from the people of Frederick and the surrounding area—or until McClellan began his advance. He also awaited former governor Enoch Lowe, an ardent Southern supporter, who was thought to have great influence with the people of western Maryland. Since Governor Lowe did not arrive, Lee decided on the eighth to issue a proclamation to the people of Maryland. This document was undoubtedly prepared by Colonel Charles Marshall of his staff, a native of Baltimore. Its tone may be gathered from the following closing sentences:

> *No restrain upon your free will is intended. No intimidation will be allowed. This army will respect your choice whatever it may be; and while the Southern people will rejoice to welcome you to your natural position among them, they will only welcome you when you come of your own will.*[9]

Maryland read with respect the proclamation of General Lee, inviting them to make free choice between North and South. But Maryland remained calm and stayed in the Union.

Lee had supposed that the advance upon Fredericktown would lead the Union forces to evacuate Martinsburg and Harpers Ferry, thus opening the line of communication through the Shenandoah Valley. Since this did not occur, it became necessary to dislodge the Union troops from those positions. To accomplish this with the least delay, Jackson was directed to proceed with his command to Martinsburg and, after driving the enemy from that place, to move down the south side of the Potomac on Harpers Ferry. General Lafayette McLaws, with his own and General R.H. Anderson's division, was ordered to seize Maryland Heights, on the north side of the Potomac opposite Harpers Ferry, and General Walker to take possession of Loudoun Heights, on the east side of the Shenandoah where it unites with the Potomac. These several commands were directed, after reducing Harpers Ferry and clearing the valley of Union forces, to join the rest of the army at Boonsboro or Hagerstown. This was Lee's Order No. 191, later to become famous as the "Lost Order."[10]

Visits to Fredericktown, shopping, Lee's proclamation to the people of Maryland and the formulation of Order No. 191 made September 8 a big day. That night, there was a lighter moment.

Jeb Stuart's cavalry was south of Frederick, screening and protecting the army. In the quaint village of Urbana there was a female academy at Landon Hall. Jeb Stuart, always fond of music and dancing, decided to have a dance or a ball for his troops.

Colonel William Willis Blackford of his staff said that the general wanted to hold the dance in gratitude for the kindness and hospitality of the people of Urbana. A large room in the school was decorated with regimental flags. And as darkness fell, people began to arrive. The cavalrymen came prepared for any emergency but put their sabers aside while they prepared to "dance the night away."[11]

Soon the ball was interrupted. McClellan's advance guard had struck a cavalry outpost. The troopers hastily gathered their weapons, mounted their steeds and galloped off into the night.

Soon wounded troopers were brought back. Young ladies in their finest attire now became nurses. Most of the wounds were minor, and one trooper said that he would get hit any day if he could have such lovely nurses. The hours ticked away, and at last the troopers and the belles bid one another a fond farewell. It was a night never to be forgotten.[12]

Reflecting on his time in Frederick, John Chamberlayne, a Confederate officer, wrote to his sister saying that the residents of Frederick were generally kind. "However, they fear us…but many of them seem to think us Goths and vandals." He also noted that "the valley of the Monocacy is beautiful" and added: "This county, Frederick, is as Yankee as Hartford or Cape Cod." He expressed the fact that he was lonesome and missed his books and familiar faces.

Long before daylight on Wednesday, September 10, the Army of Northern Virginia struck its campsites at Monocacy Junction and Worman's Mill. Each command was moving to carry out its respective assignment in Order No. 191.

Thomas J. Jackson rode into town and turned left onto West Second Street. He hoped to pay a quick visit to Reverend Ross, pastor of the Presbyterian church. However, at 5:30 a.m. the clergyman was still asleep, so Jackson rode on and rejoined his command where Bentz Street intersects with West Patrick Street.[13]

The Presbyterian
church. *Author's collection.*

Jed Hotchkiss reports leaving camp at 3:00 a.m. Along the route of
march, he found strong Union sentiment, but all of the folks were amazed
and thankful for the discipline of the Confederate troops.[14]

A lady wrote a classic description of the appearance of the Army of
Northern Virginia in Frederick:

> *I wish, my dear Minnie, you could have witnessed the transit of the
> Rebel army through our streets…Their coming was unheralded by any
> pomp and pageant whatever. No burst of martial music greeted your ear,
> no thundering sound of cannon, no bill staff no glittering cortege dashed
> through the streets: Instead came three long, dirty columns that kept on
> In an unceasing flow. I could scarcely believe my eyes: was this body of*

men moving so smoothly along, with no order, their guns carried in every fashion, no two dressed alike, their officers hardly distinguishable from the privates, were these, I asked myself in amazement, were these dirty, lank ugly specimens of humanity, with hocks of hair sticking through holes in their hats, and dust thick in their dirty faces, the men that had coped and encountered successfully, and driven back again and again, our splendid legions with their fine discipline, their martial show and color, their solid battalions keeping such perfect time to the inspiring bands of music?

Why it seemed as if a single regiment of our gallant boys in blue could drive that dirty crew into the river without any trouble. And then, too. I wish you could see how they behaved—a crowd of boys on a holiday don't seem happier. They are on the broad grin all the time. O, they are so dirty! I don't think the Potomac River could wash them clean: and ragged! There is not a scare crow in our cornfields that would not scorn to exchange clothes with them: and so tattered! There isn't a decently dressed soldier in the whole army.

I saw some strikingly handsome faces though, or rather they would have been so if they could have had a good scrubbing. They were very polite, I must confess, and always asked for a drink of water, or anything else, and never think of coming inside of a door without an invitation. Many of them were bare footed indeed. I felt sorry for the poor, misguided wretches, for some of them limped along so painfully, trying to keep up with their comrades.[15]

Yet those grimy, sweaty, lean, ragged men were the flower of Lee's army. But they were soldiers and well disciplined. Even a Union sympathizer wrote in admiration:

In manners, in the conduct of soldiers and the discipline, these bundles of rags, these cough-racked, diseased and starved men excel our well-fed, well-clothed, our best soldiers. No one can point to a single act of vandalism perpetrated by the Rebel soldiery during their occupation of Frederick. while even now a countless host of [Federal] stragglers are crawling after our own army, devouring, destroying or wasting all that falls in their devious line of march. God knows I have no need to praise Confederate forebearance, but the fact that we are confronted by an army perfectly under the control and discipline of tried and experienced officers incontrovertible. It accounts for the excellence of their fighting, and the almost powerlessness of our own army.[16]

Jacob Engelbrecht described what it was like on West Patrick Street:

Going—perhaps Gone—This morning say 3 or 4 o'clock Southern Army, commenced moving westward and have continued ever since (now 10 hours) and still passing through town from the George town road…I suppose 50 or 60 thousand men and several hundred cannon.[17]

At 3:00 a.m. on the morning of the eleventh, Jacob wrote again:

Still Marching—the passing of the Rebel troops Continued all day yesterday, until night & this morning about three hours more…It took them about 17 hours altogether—we estimate the whole number at about seventy thousand…at least 1000 wagons & ambulances—very few Cavalry— only those that came the first day. I saw Nearly the whole of them pass— thinking I would never see the like again—they were generally young and hearty…Many were barefooted and some had one Shoe & one barefoot— they really looked "Ragged and tough." The first 8 or 10 thousand got a tolerable good supply of Clothing & Shoes & boots but the Stores & Shops were soon sold out & the whole town was with closed doors and windows (This was from Saturday to Thursday). I suppose the length of the whole Cavalcade wagons—Cannon & men would make a string of about 14 or 16 miles—I was very anxious to see the whole proceedings of an enemy taking a town…I must say that at no time was I the least alarmed… We took it cooly & deliberately…We put ourselves into the hands of the Lord who had watched over us so many years & we were fully assured he would not forsake us in the time of Need…I must say the Rebels behaved themselves well…Our town is as still & quiet as a Sabbath day.[18]

It was during this westward movement that the Barbara Fritchie incident is supposed to have occurred.

Robert E. Lee rode through the streets of Frederick in an ambulance. In early September, he had stepped on his poncho while preparing to mount his horse Traveler. Throwing his hands out to break his fall, he

The Barbara Fritchie House. *Frederick County Archives.*

apparently broke one wrist and sprained another. His troops, seeing him in an ambulance, thought that it was an ill omen.

Prior to departing Frederick, John Dooley of the Eighth Virginia made a hasty visit to the Catholic school in Frederick. He caused an anxious moment for Father Ward. Some paroled Union prisoners had also come to the school seeking food and shelter. At least, though, John was leaving Frederick a clean man. Earlier, the priest had taken pity on John as he beheld the dirty, tattered uniform. The priest insisted on giving him clean clothing, complete with underwear. John was ready to march, feeling like a new man, clean all over.[19]

As the Stonewall Brigade marched past the Markell home on West Patrick Street, a young lady gave Henry Douglas a pretty Rebel flag. Not to be outdone, Mrs. Markell pinned a small Confederate flag to the hat of a South Carolina soldier.[20]

As Jackson ascended the eastern slope of Catoctin Mountain, he rode with Abner Hopkins, chaplain of the Stonewall Brigade. Lamenting the losses at Second Manassas, he inquired of the chaplain if he felt those who had died were ready to meet their maker.[21]

The long gray column, with the exception of John Walker, entered the Middletown Valley. Walker had retraced his steps to make an attempt to destroy a part of the Chesapeake and Ohio Canal. In Middletown,

Lafayette McClaws turned toward Burkittsville and Crampton's Gap. The rest of the army continued westward toward Boonsboro.

The Confederates departed Frederick on Wednesday, September 10, to carry out the objectives of Lee's Order No. 191. By Friday, September 12, the leading elements of the Army of the Potomac were fast approaching the "clustered spires of Fredericktown." McClellan had organized his command into three wings. The wing to the far right, following what is now basically Maryland Route 97, was commanded by Ambrose Burnside. It consisted of the First and Ninth Corps and, after striking the Baltimore Pike, advanced to New Market and proceeded to Frederick.

The center wing of the Army of the Potomac, consisting of the Second and newly formed Twelfth Corps commanded by Major General Edwin Sumner, advanced on the main road from Frederick to Washington, as well as via Damascus and Ijamsville. William Franklin with the Sixth Corps advanced on the river road, now largely Maryland Route 28, toward Buckeystown.

Friday, September 12, was a warm autumn day with an occasional shower. The Army of Northern Virginia continued on its mission to capture Harpers Ferry. Meanwhile, the Army of the Potomac was converging on Frederick. About thirty-five thousand Confederates had passed through Frederick. Now eighty thousand men in blue were converging on the city. Between thirty thousand and forty thousand horses and mules pulled the supply wagons, ambulances, the cannons and caissons of the two armies. There were also the mounts of the officers and cavalry.

Wade Hampton and a contingent of Confederate cavalry remained in Frederick. However, at about 5:00 p.m., Alfred Pleasonton and troopers in blue entered Frederick from the direction of Urbana. Hampton's men retreated from the area of Mount Olivet Cemetery toward the square. Jacob Engelbrecht and others went to the rooftops and watched the unfolding drama with opera glasses.[22]

The Confederates retreated to Bentz Street and then reformed and galloped east toward the square with sabers drawn. There was a lot of noise and commotion with the horses and sabers. Some troopers on both sides were cut, but there were few serious casualties.

Meanwhile, elements of the Ninth Corps were advancing on the Baltimore Road from New Market. Isaac Rodman's division advanced on the double quick, tearing down fences and moving through cornfields. Confederates, seeing the massed colors of the advancing infantry from the east, broke off the engagement and retreated toward Catoctin Mountain. The smell of powder remained in the air.

As the Ninth Corps entered Frederick, the members received a joyous welcome. Windows were thrown open, and cheers for the Union and the men in blue filled the air. Flags and red, white and blue bunting were displayed.

Ambrose Burnside, the right wing commander, and Jesse Lee Reno, the Ninth Corps commander, had difficulty getting into Frederick. Their path was blocked by adoring residents. Burnside and Reno stopped for a while at the Wayside Inn on East Patrick Street.

For the men in blue, this was the first evening since the beginning of the war they had been in friendly territory. Previously they had been in Virginia or the Carolinas, where they had been met with frowns and insults. Now they were being received as heroes and were looked on as deliverers.

Charles Johnson and David Thompson were members of the Ninth New York Zouaves, a unit begun by Colonel Rush Hawkins, one of the founders of Brown University. Johnson said, "The cheering exceeded anything I ever heard. Frederick was a lovely and loyal city."[23] David Thompson, a former schoolteacher in Flushing, New York, said, "The experience in Frederick was a bright one…the topic of discussion at many a campfire for months to come." Camp was made near the old jail. One of the soldiers slipped out and returned to camp with a crock of apple butter, bread, a skillet and a live hen. Soon the men were feasting on chicken.[24]

Lieutenants Barnett and Horner also spent part of the evening in Frederick. Returning to camp, they spotted a fire at the jail and sounded the alarm. Several companies of the Ninth quickly became firemen and guards, assisting in firefighting and also preventing the escape of the convicts.

At the dawn of a lovely September 13, Lee and Longstreet were at Hagerstown responding to the threat of a Union advance from Pennsylvania. Lafayette McLaws was moving on Maryland Heights, seeking to dislodge Union troops from their position, while Stonewall Jackson was moving on Harpers Ferry.

Barbara Fritchie's grave. *Author's collection.*

The Union Ninth Corps was in the eastern portion of Frederick, while the rest of the Army of the Potomac was just south of the city, near Urbana and Monocacy Junction. Alfred Pleasonton's cavalry was nipping at the heels of the Confederate horsemen. There was skirmishing at Hagan's Gap, just west of Frederick. Farther to the west, Daniel Harvey Hill, with the brigades of Samuel Garland and Robert Rodes, were acting as a rear guard for the Confederate army at Fox's and Turnery's Passes, the latter on the National Road. Jeb Stuart and his cavalry were at Crampton's Gap.

For the Army of the Potomac, this was a joyous day—smiles, hugs, food and drink and a great reception. David Strother, a member of McClellan's staff, wrote:

We were welcomed with a spontaneous ovation that stirred every soul to the depths. The whole city was fluttering with national flags…it seemed as though the entire population had turned out, wild with joy. Handkerchiefs, flags, etc. were waved and showered upon the troops. Crowds gathered around General McClellan. "Little Dan," the General's horse, was covered with floral wreaths. [25]

The enthusiastic crowd brought McClellan and his staff to a halt. Later, he wrote to his wife:

I can't describe for you…the enthusiastic welcome reception we met with at…Frederick. I was nearly overwhelmed and pulled to pieces. I enclose…a little flag that some lady thrust into Dan's bridle…I was seldom more affected by the scenes I saw…and the reception I met with…men, women, and children crowded around us weeping, shouting and praying. [26]

David Strother was amazed at how well the Confederate army behaved and acted while in Frederick. Strother noted that they had "acted better than ours." [27]

While McClellan was riding triumphantly through the streets of Frederick, one of the war's most dramatic events was occurring south of Fredericktown. Elements of the Twelfth Corps, including the Twenty-seventh Indiana, made camp on grounds formerly occupied by the Confederates.

Shortly after the men began pitching their tents, Sergeant John M. Bloss and Private Barton W. Mitchell found three cigars. Wrapped around the cigar was a piece of paper. It was a copy of Lee's Order No. 191, detailing the routes and objectives of the Army of Northern Virginia. Realizing its possible importance, Mitchell and Bloss took it to Captain Peter Kop, the commander of Company D. It went up the chain of command. [28]

McClellan then showed those present the copy of Order No. 191. He was elated. He said that he knew Lee's plans and that if the men did their job, he could pitch into the Confederate center and destroy the Confederate army. McClellan also promised Gibbon the next western regiment to add to the troops from Wisconsin and Indiana. Gibbon rode back to camp in better spirits "than I had had in a month," feeling that at last the army had a commander to stand against the likes of Lee and Jackson.[29]

It was early afternoon. There were several hours of daylight, as well as good marching weather. The situation called for rapid movement and for McClellan to move quickly and interpose between the divided elements of the Army of Northern Virginia. However, rapidity of movement was not in McClellan's vocabulary. Thus, he did little but begin to funnel the Ninth Corps into the Middletown Valley.

On Saturday afternoon, Dame Barbara Fritchie, living on West Patrick Street, had a visitor. It was none other than Jesse Lee Reno. For whatever reason, the general stopped at the Fritchie home. The aged Barbara gave him a glass of wine. General Reno also sat at her desk and wrote a letter home. It would be his last. She also gave him a flag. Then the general departed.

Harper's Weekly image of McClellan in Frederick.

General Reno was born in Ohio, near Wheeling, West Virginia, on June 20, 1823. He graduated from West Point in 1846 in the class with George B. McClellan and Thomas J. Jackson. He won honors for bravery in the Mexican-American War and was an expert in the field of ordnance. At the outbreak of hostilities, he was in command at the Mount Vernon Arsenal in Alabama. Regretfully, he had to surrender U.S. property to the State of Alabama. Reno had also taught ordnance at West Point. The city of Reno, Nevada, is named for the general.

Amid the gala reception, Jonathan Letterman, the medical director of the army, knew that there would soon be need of major hospitals. Thus he took the time to ride around Frederick to select hospital sites. Naturally, these would be the largest buildings. In addition to the grounds at the Hessian barracks, Letterman selected most of the churches.

As twilight came, "a hundred circling camps" surrounded Frederick. Smoke from campfires spiraled skyward. The troops prepared their evening meal and coffee. They spoke of the enthusiastic reception afforded them in Frederick.

Colonel Gordon of the Second Massachusetts, along with Lieutenant Colonel Wilder Dwight and Chaplain Quint, remained in the city with friends they had made the previous winter. Earlier in the day, Dwight had sought a physician to lance a boil.

The clock on the tower of Trinity Chapel ticked away the last seconds and minutes of September 13. The residents of Frederick had never seen a day like it, and the men in blue had precious memories that would last a lifetime.

Next came Sunday, September 14, 1862. The camps of the Union army were astir early on the morning of the September Sabbath. The Ninth Corps, near Middletown, was preparing to attack Confederate positions at Fox's Gap. Meanwhile, from camps ringing Fredericktown, the various corps of the army began the march that led to Antietam. The First Corps plodded through the streets of Frederick, taking the National Road, now Alternate Route 40, crossing Catoctin Mountain and moving toward Turner's Gap. They were followed by the Second Corps and then the Twelfth, which consisted of the reserve of the army. Soldiers wrote home or inscribed in journals the emotional reception given the Army of the Potomac.

Rufus Dawes was a native of Ohio who migrated to Wisconsin. September found him as an officer in the Sixth Wisconsin Volunteers. Writing of his experience in Frederick, Dawes said:

Our camp on this quiet Sabbath morning...was in the valley of Monocacy near Frederick...there is no fairer landscape in our country...the day was bright, warm, and clear. The bells of the city of Frederick were all ringing...the spires of the city were glistening in the morning sunlight.

At eight o'clock...our brigade marched forward. The Sixth Wisconsin was in advance. Our entry was triumphal. The stars and stripes floated from every building. The joyful people thronged the streets to greet the veterans of the Army of the Potomac. Little children stood at nearly every door, freely offering cool water, cakes, pies, and dainties.[30]

John Gibbon, a former artillery instructor at West Point, now commanding a brigade in the First Corps, had roots in Baltimore. Reflecting the division of families is the fact that several of his brothers fought for the Confederacy. However, John was also pleased with the warm welcome in Frederick.

Before coming to Frederick, Gibbon did not believe that there was much Union sentiment in the city. He was pleasantly surprised by the reception, complete with flags, food and adoring residents. He thought the response had not been seen since the days of George Washington: "The same feeling has also been exhibited toward us. All along the road the people all come out to speak to us as we pass and show their delight... there is no question of the loyalty of this part of Maryland."[31]

The Second Corps commanded by the aged Edwin Vose Sumner followed the First Corps. Members of the command later shared their reflections on the September Sabbath.

Frank Sawyer enjoyed marching through Frederick, "a most beautiful town." Like the others, he dwelled on the welcome in his memoirs, but added, "the men were almost wild with enthusiasm. [They] had not seen a woman's face that wore a smile in a year." However, the Virginians had not been happy to have Yankees on their soil. One of the Ohioans shouted, "We're *in* God's country again!"

Jonathan P. Stowe, from Grafton, Massachusetts, was thirty years old in September 1862 and a member of the Fifteenth Massachusetts Infantry. He noted that the day was very hot and that there was much suffering from the heat and thirst.[32]

That morning, he woke at 3:00 a.m. and had some coffee. By daylight, he and his comrades were on their way to Frederick. At 9:00 a.m.,

Harper's Weekly image of troop movements.

they apparently reached Monocacy Junction. An hour later, General McClellan passed amid deafening cheers. The Rebs had lived in the area for a week. Stowe said, "They slew lots of cattle." At noon, Jacob H. Cole, a member of the Fifty-seventh New York, also noted a delightful experience on this pleasant Saturday in mid-September:

> *It was a welcome change also to be greeted with smiles Instead of frowns. Probably no soldier who entered Frederick City on the morning of September 13th will ever forget the cordial welcome with which the rescuing army was received by the local inhabitants.*[33]
>
> *Monocacy, shut in by low mountains of surprising grace of outline, all nature was in bloom. The signs of comfort and opulence met the eye on every side, while as the full brigades of Sumner marched in perfect order and with all the pomp of war, with glittering staff and proud commanders, old Sumner at the head, pressed through the quaint and beautiful town, the streets resounded with applause and from balcony and windows fair faces smiled and handkerchiefs and scarf's waved to greet the army of the Union. Many an honest and many a fair*

countenance of patriotic men and women looked out upon the brave array of Sumner's corps with smiles and tears of gratitude and Joy. Amid all that was desolate and gloomy, amid all that was harsh and terrible in the service, that these soldiers of the Union were called to render that bright day of September 13th, 1862, still that gracious scene of natural beauty and waving crops that quaint and charming southern city, that friendly greeting form a picture which can never pass out of the memory of those whose fortune it was to enter Frederick town that day.[34]

The veterans of the Fifth New Hampshire noted that the residents of Frederick had a polite but restrained response to the Confederate occupation but looked upon the men in blue "as valiant liberators." As the men from New Hampshire approached the cheering throngs, they braced up with pride as though they were marching by in review. The national and regimental colors were unfurled, and each man quickened his step. The proud soldier's pulse quickened. Like other writers, Thomas Livermore says that flags and bunting were everywhere. Women were on the street and peering from every window waving flags and handkerchiefs. There were bright smiles everywhere. Livermore noted, "There had been no moment as splendid since the men left New Hampshire."[35]

Among those marching on Patrick Street were two future presidents. Both were members of the Twenty-third Ohio Volunteers. It was the only time in history that two men who would serve in the White House were in the same military unit at the same time. Rutherford B. Hayes was the lieutenant colonel of the regiment. He was severely wounded at Fox's Gap on September 14, almost bleeding to death. Taken to Middletown to a private home, he was treated and recovered. Driving the commissary wagon was the nineteen-year-old commissary sergeant, William B. McKinley. He won a battlefield commission on the heights above Burnside Bridge, serving his comrades food and drink while under fire. A large monument stands on the site. McKinley returned on May 30, 1900, to dedicate the Maryland Monument.

The September Sabbath brought the first major battle fought on Maryland soil. At about nine o'clock in the morning, the Ninth Corps advanced on Fox's Gap. They met with success. But late morning halted their attack. In the ensuing hours, both armies hastened additional troops toward South Mountain. By late afternoon, more than twenty-four hours after the finding of Order No. 191, McClellan was ready to attack and strike the South Mountain passes.

The First Corps under Joseph Hooker advanced on Turner's Gap via the Mount Tabor and National Roads. John Gibbon with his troops from Wisconsin and Indiana, along with Battery B, was on the National Road. Three miles south, the Ninth Corps was ready to attack Fox's Gap. And farther south, near the village of Burkittsville, William B. Franklin and the Union Sixth Corps began advancing on Crampton's Gap, the mountain pass nearest Harpers Ferry.

There was heavy fighting. Some say that it "was fire on mountain"; more than 2,300 men in blue were killed, wounded or listed as missing. The Confederate loss was listed at 3,434.

The men of the Twelfth Corps reached Bolivar on the National Road west of Middletown. As darkness descended, they spotted an ambulance and a detachment of cavalry headed east. They questioned who was in the ambulance. It was Major General Jesse Lee Reno, who had been mortally wounded at sunset. He expired under an oak tree and was being taken to Frederick. The soldiers looked on this as an ill omen and lamented his loss.[36]

Robert E. Lee said, "The day has gone against us." He sent couriers into the darkness with orders for the army to come together on the hills of Sharpsburg near Antietam Creek.

At dawn on Monday, September 15, half of the Army of Northern Virginia began to take up positions on the ridges between the villa of Sharpsburg and Antietam Creek.

While this was happening, Jackson, with the other half of the Confederate army, bombarded Union positions at Harpers Ferry and then advanced with his infantry. Shortly, a white flag was seen, and the Union garrison surrendered. This was the largest capitulation of American troops until the fall of Bataan and Corregidor in the spring of 1942.

Jackson said that he would hasten his command to Sharpsburg. However, it would take more than forty-eight hours to disengage, cross the Potomac and join Lee.

For the moment, Lee stood alone, but McClellan did not move aggressively. The next day, fog enshrouded the hills of Sharpsburg.

Major General Jesse Lee Reno.
Library of Congress.

It was the lull before the storm, "the gathering of the hosts" and the marshalling of thousands of troops. It was also the eve of the seventy-fifth anniversary of the signing of the Constitution. Some soldiers from Connecticut wondered if by the next evening there would be a United States of America at all.

With the dawn of the seventeenth, the earth began to shake. Shot and shell filled the air. The battle to continue the existence of the nation raged in D.R. Miller's cornfield, in the East and West Woods, around a white brick church, at a sunken road later renamed Bloody Lane and south of town at a stone bridge. Lee's army was saved only by the seventeen-mile march of A.P. Hill from Harpers Ferry.

The sun went down on America's bloodiest day. Yes, there were 51,000 casualties in three days at Gettysburg and 6,800 at the beaches of Normandy. But at Antietam, there were 12,410 Union casualties and 10,700 Confederate; 5,000 were killed outright, and at least another 1,000 would die from their wounds. Doctors of both armies treated the wounded "by dim and flaring lamps." The area was "one vast hospital," with 18,000 lads from the North and South being treated.

Technically, the battle was a draw. However, Lee recrossed the Potomac on the night of September 18, and the North claimed victory. Maryland remained in the Union, England and France withheld diplomatic and economic assistance and Lincoln and the Republicans maintained control of the government.

However, there was an even greater significance. During the summer, Lincoln had prayed for a victory, and Antietam was considered a Union victory. He therefore on September 22 announced that on January 1, 1863, he would declare the slaves in the rebellious states free. Thus, the scope and purpose of the war was broadened. It had been fought to save the Union. Now, it was also being fought to abolish slavery. Antietam (or Sharpsburg) is etched forever in the annals of history, and the troops of the Army of Northern Virginia and the Army of the Potomac marched through Frederick en route to that epic struggle.

Despite Lincoln's urgings, the bulk of the Army of the Potomac remained in the Antietam Valley until the end of October. There

Fence rails disappeared. *Author's collection.*

were thousands to be fed. Medical supplies were needed for the many hospitals in and around the battlefield. Thus, trains bearing blankets, tents, food, medicine and other military items arrived at Monocacy Junction every day.

At the junction, the supplies were off-loaded onto wagons. From there, the teams of horses or mules pulled the wagons into Frederick and then west on Patrick Street and across the mountains to Sharpsburg.

Most of the time, after the supplies were distributed, the wagons were loaded with the recovering wounded to be returned to Frederick to one of the larger hospitals or to be sent home via the railroad.

A rest stop was made at Zion Lutheran Church in Middletown. There, within the confines of the church, the soldiers were given food and drink. Then the trips to Frederick was resumed.

In early October, President Lincoln had urged McClellan to follow Lee and strike him before winter set in. The general, however, had excuse after excuse and kept most of the army near Sharpsburg until October 26. The Second and Twelfth Corps were already at Harpers Ferry. Proceeding to Berlin—now Brunswick, Maryland—the rest of the army crossed the Potomac and headed south toward Lovettsville and Warrenton.

Being a very pragmatic leader, and keenly aware of McClellan's popularity with his troops, Lincoln waited until two days after the November election to change commanders.

On November 7, an early autumn snowstorm struck the Northeast. The wind howled, and the air was filled with snowflakes. Lincoln and Henry Halleck had had enough.

Although the weather was fit for neither man or beast, a Union officer was riding through the stormy night. It was C. Putnam Buckingham. He had graduated from West Point in the class with Robert E. Lee. The year 1862 found him on special duty with the War Department. In his dispatch pouch he had special orders for Burnside.

After finding Burnside's tent and awakening him, Buckingham handed him General Order No. 182. The order announced the removal of George B. McClellan from the command of the Army of the Potomac and the appointment of Ambrose P. Burnside as his replacement. The colonel, who had been in Frederick in June 1861, was now the commander of one of the largest armies in the world.

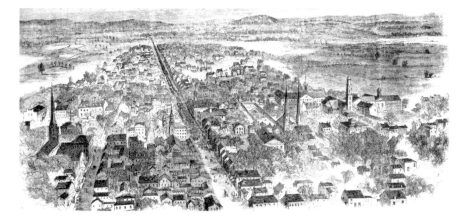

Harper's Weekly image of Frederick, 1862.

The officer from Rhode Island was in shock. But being a military man, he accepted his orders, moving with clarity. The army marched toward Fredericksburg, Virginia. That city had the misfortune to be midway between Washington and Richmond. The first of several Civil War battles loomed on the horizon.

Burnside planned to attack Fredericksburg before the Army of Northern Virginia farther to the west could reach the hills south of the city. Sadly, for him, the boats that were to hold the pontoon bridges were late in arriving. Therefore, the Union crossing of the Rappahannock was delayed, and Lee was able to get between Burnside and Richmond.

On December 13, Burnside launched his attack on Fredericksburg. It was a disaster, a debacle. Union troops crossed the river and struck the Confederates on Marye's Heights along a fortified line. The losses in the Army of the Potomac were appalling.

Chapter 5

HAIL TO THE CHIEF

It was Wednesday morning, October 1, 1862, two weeks after the Battle of Antietam. At 6:00 a.m., a train departed from Washington, destination Harpers Ferry, Virginia. West Virginia was not yet a state. On board were Mr. John Garrett, the president of the Baltimore & Ohio Railroad; Ward Hill Lamon, the marshal of the District of Columbia; Ozias Hatch, an Illinois politician; and none other than President Abraham Lincoln. The purpose of the trip was to thank the troops for their gallantry at Antietam and to confer with George B. McClellan, the commander of the Army of the Potomac. The objective was to get McClellan to begin chasing Robert E. Lee, who was in the Shenandoah Valley.

The train reached Harpers Ferry at noon. The presidential party left the train on the Maryland side of the Potomac and crossed the river on a pontoon bridge. There were some conferences and a review of the troops. On October 2, Lincoln visited Union encampments on Loudoun and Maryland Heights. Then it was on to the Antietam Valley.

On October 3, Lincoln reviewed almost the entire army, toured the battlefield, posed for pictures at the home of Stephen P. Grove, west of Sharpsburg, and had extensive talks with McClellan.

Then came Saturday morning, October 4, 1862; Lincoln departed McClellan's headquarters on the Mills Road south of Sharpsburg and rode into Sharpsburg in a coach pulled by two white horses. Heading east on what is now Maryland Route 34, a little boy by the name of Frisby Keplinger appeared and gave the president a cup of cold water.

After crossing the Middle Bridge over Antietam Creek, the column turned into the farm of Phillip Pry. The Pry farm had been McClellan's headquarters September 15 through September 20. Lincoln was coming to visit the wounded General Israel B. Richardson, a patient in an upstairs bed.

The president, accompanied by General McClellan and staff, rode to Boonsboro and then to South Mountain. The commander took some time to show Mr. Lincoln portions of the South Mountain battlefield.

For years, there was a question as to Lincoln's route from Antietam to Frederick. The answer was discovered just a few years ago by a Washington County resident, Ed Itnrye. He found an October 10, 1862 edition of the *Middletown Valley Register*. The newspaper carried this account:

> *Last week President Lincoln accompanied by General McClellan and staff...returned to Washington, via Boonsboro, Middletown and Frederick...Gen. McClellan and staff accompanied the party within two miles of this place* [Middletown] *where they took leave of the President and returned to headquarters. An enthusiastic welcome was given the President in Frederick.*[1]

Riding with Mr. Lincoln into Frederick were Captains I.S. Marther and Derrickson, of McClellan's staff. At the western edge of Frederick, an artillery battery fired a presidential salute. In some manner, the residents of Frederick discovered that the president was coming. West Patrick Street was thronged with people waiting to get a glimpse of him.

Just prior to his arrival, there was a light shower and a strong wind, but by 5:00 p.m. the weather had cleared. The crowd was not deterred by the temporary inconvenience. Colonel Allen, the military governor of Frederick, greeted the president. A small detachment of the First Maine Cavalry joined the procession.

The presidential party proceeded to Record Street, where Mr. Lincoln visited General Hartsuff at the Ramsay House. The officer had been wounded at the Battle of South Mountain.

A large crowd gathered outside the Ramsay House, including many blacks. In fact, Lincoln gave eight-year-old Alice Frazier a paper note. A little later, the cook sent Alice to a nearby store to purchase five cents worth of snuff. Walking wounded from the nearby Presbyterian church also gathered in the street, seeking to catch a glimpse of Father Abraham.[2]

Harper's Weekly image of Lincoln's train in Frederick.

The visit to Frederick was short. Jacob Engelbrecht, the erstwhile journalist, noted: "The President staid [*sic*] in town only about half an hour." However, according to newspapers, in this time he made two brief speeches. The first occurred when he came out the front door of the Ramsay House. The folks assembled in the street called for a speech. The president had little to say.

> *In my present position it is hardly proper for me to make speeches every word is so closely noted that it will not do to make a foolish one, and I cannot be expected to be prepared to make a sensible one. If I were as I have been most of my life, I might perhaps talk nonsense to you for half an hour, wouldn't hurt anyone. As it is, I can only return thanks for the compliments paid our cause. Please accept my sincere thanks for the compliments paid our cause. Please accept my sincere thanks for the compliments to our Country.*[3]

Mr. Lincoln then reentered the ambulance and was driven to the railroad station, closely followed by the rapidly increasing crowd. The party immediately entered the handsomely fitted cars, which had been in readiness for nearly forth-eight hours. The president was again loudly called by the throng of citizens and soldiers, and upon making his appearance another speech was demanded. He good-naturedly responded:

> *I am surrounded by soldiers, and a lie farther off by the citizens of this good city of Frederick. Nevertheless I can only say, as I did five minutes ago, it is not proper for me to make speeches in my present condition. I return thanks to our good soldiers for the services they have rendered, the energy they have shown, the hardships they have endured, and the blood they have shed for this Union of ours; and I also return thanks, not only to the soldiers, but to the good citizens of Frederick, and to the good men, women, and children in this land of ours, for their devotion in the glorious cause, and I say this with no malice in my heart to those who have done otherwise. May our children and children's children for a thousand generations enjoy these benefits conferred upon us by a united country, and have cause yet to rejoice under these glorious institutions, bequeathed to us by Washington and his compeers. Now, my friends, soldiers and citizens, I can only say once more, farewell.*[4]

Lincoln then entered the rear of the car "amid acclamations of the crowd," and the train moved off. As the people cheered, Lincoln emerged again and waved his hat. In fact, he stood on the rear platform of the car and waved until the crowd disappeared from view.

Like those who assembled later at Gettysburg, the residents of Frederick City and Frederick County would long remember the brief visit of Mr. Lincoln, his appearance and his words.

Chapter 6

DAME BARBARA FRITCHIE

No story of Frederick in the Civil War would be complete without an account of Barbara Fritchie. There is no question of the fact that she was a resident of Frederick, living on West Patrick Street, but the question of waving the flag in the face of mighty Stonewall is debatable, considering Jackson did not ride past her home.

Barbara Hauer Fritchie was born near Lancaster, Pennsylvania, on December 3, 1766. Thus she lived during our war for independence. She was the daughter of John Niclaus and Catherine Zeller Hauer. Shortly after Barbara's birth, the family moved to Frederick.

On May 18, 1806, at the age of forty, she married John Caspar Fritchie, fourteen years her junior. Their marriage lasted until November 10, 1849, when Mr. Fritchie passed away.

Barbara reached the advanced age of ninety-five. Apparently, she remained very alert and was a staunch Unionist and very much antislavery. She was filled with anxiety when the Confederates occupied Frederick, but the worst was yet to come. On Wednesday, September 10, more than thirty thousand men in gray, along with their supply wagons and cannons, went right by her home. The Army of Northern Virginia was moving in compliance with Lee's Order No. 191 to take Harpers Ferry.

Most of Jackson's command, except A.P. Hill's division and "Stonewall" himself, passed the Fritchie home. Jackson was a friend of Reverend and Mrs. Ross and stopped there on the morning of the tenth to bid them farewell. Reverend Ross was the pastor of the Presbyterian church. The preacher's home was on West Second Street, so Jackson, after stopping there, rode down Bentz Street and rejoined his command at the intersection of West Patrick Street, which is just a short distance west of the Fritchie home.

The next two paragraphs are taken from Miss Eleanor D. Abbott's book on Barbara Fritchie. Miss Abbott was a great-grandniece of "Dame Barbara" and had in her home, opposite the Maryland State School for the Deaf, many of Barbara Fritchie's possessions:

Further confirmation of the flag waving incident is found on page seven of the April 8, 1910 issue of the Atlanta Constitution, a Southern publication, on file in the Congressional Library, Washington, D.C. It comes from the Confederate Captain Frank Meyers, who was at that time a sergeant in the 6th Virginia. He tells that Barbara Fritchie came out on her porch and waved her little flag at them as they were passing her house, and one of the soldiers called to him: "Sergeant, let me shoot it down." Captain Meyers said, "I told him 'no,' as we had been given positive orders not to disturb a thing in the town"; so not one of them bothered her.[1]

Mrs. Fritchie's own account of the incident, as told to a niece, goes something like this:

It was early morning, September 10, 1862. The large bunting flag had not yet been placed in the dormer window, as it was not quite seven o'clock. One of Mrs. Hanshew's children came in, calling excitedly, "Look out for your flag, the troops are coming!" [Mrs. Hanshew had heard the Confederates were en route through the town, and had sent the child to warn her aunt not to display the flag, but she misunderstood.] *Thinking the Union troops were coming, Mrs. Fritchie took her small silk flag from between the leaves of the family Bible and stepped out on the front porch. Immediately one of the men came to her and told her she had better go in, or she might be harmed. Realizing her mistake, and that she was in the midst of Confederate soldiers, she nevertheless refused to go in. Then a second soldier came and tried to take the flag from her, saying he wanted to put it on his horse's head. A third soldier threatened to shoot it out of her hand if she didn't go in. An officer rode forward, turned angrily upon the man and said, "If you harm a hair on that old lady's head I'll shoot you down like a dog." Then turning to the trembling old lady, he said, "Go on, Granny, wave your flag as much as you please." A little after seven o'clock, when her companion, Miss Yoner, went to call her to breakfast she found Mrs. Fritchie in the parlor quite excited, "They tried to take my flag, but a man would not let them; and he was a gentleman."[2]*

Barbara Fritchie herself told the above account to Miss Caroline Ebert, her husband's niece, who came to see her shortly after the flag-waving incident. In 1913, as plans were being made to erect a monument in Mrs. Fritchie's honor, she related the story to Mrs. J.H. Abbott and Miss Eleanor D. Abbott and made an affidavit before a notary public.

Miss Ebert visited Washington in the fall of the year and told the story of Barbara Fritchie waving the flag to some of her friends. Mrs. E.D.E.N. Southworth, who was a noted novelist of the time, gained possession of the account and sent it to John Greenleaf Whittier, who was inspired by it and wrote the famous poem. The story, by the time it reached him, was stretched, as tales sometimes get when repeated again and again.

Barbara Fritchie celebrated her ninety-sixth birthday on December 3, 1862. Fifteen days later, the lady who was to become world famous passed away, dying from pneumonia. She was buried in the Reformed Church graveyard beside her husband. However, on May 30, 1913, their bodies were reinterred in the beautiful Mount Olivet Cemetery in Frederick, where a handsome monument in her memory was unveiled on September 9, 1914.

Following is Whittier's poem, "Barbara Fritchie":

Up from the meadows rich with corn,
Clear in the cool September morn,
The clustered spires of Frederick stand
Green-walled by the hills of Maryland

Round about them orchards sweep,
Apple and peach-tree fruited deep,
Fair as a garden of the Lord
To the eyes of the famished rebel horde.

During World War II, President Franklin D. Roosevelt met with Sir Winston Churchill at Shangri-La, now Camp David, in the Catoctin Mountains. Returning from Washington, President Roosevelt asked Sir Winston if there was any place he would like to see. He replied, "Why yes, the home of Dame Barbara Fritchie."

Until the early 1950s, there was two-way traffic on both Patrick and Market Streets. Thus, the motorcade headed south on Market Street and then turned west on Patrick, stopping in front of the Fritchie home. Tradition has it that Sir Winston Churchill, the bulldog of Great Britain, emerged from the car and quoted verbatim Whittier's famous poem.

John Greenleaf Whittier was very impressed with the church steeples of Frederick, thus he coined the phrase, "The clustered spires of Frederick." They remain a large part of Frederick's historic skyline and can be seen from high ground several miles from the east and south and west of the city.

Five steeples of four churches comprise "the clustered spires." They are Trinity Chapel, dating back to 1773 and having a 141-foot spire; Saint John's Roman Catholic spire, standing 145 feet high and dating to 1854; the twin spires of the Evangelical Lutheran Church, reaching 137 feet; and finally, the All Saints Episcopal Church's 134-foot spire.

Chapter 7

JACKSON'S STAFF

The tactics of Stonewall Jackson are studied around the world. Assisting him in carrying out the movements were the members of his staff. Three of the staff members were the sons of preachers, and each of the three had connections with Frederick. Reverend Joseph Smith and his family arrived in Frederick to serve the Presbyterian church (1838–43). Two years later, the Pendletons arrived to assume the pastorate of All Saints Episcopal Church. Henry Kyd Douglas and his parents had friends in Frederick, especially Dr. Daniel Zacharias, pastor of the German Reformed Church. Perhaps it is no surprise that Jackson, sometimes called "the Praying General," selected the sons of ministers to serve on his staff.[1]

James Power Smith, the son of the Reverend Joseph and Eliza Bell Smith, was born in Ohio on July 4, 1837. His mother was from Winchester, so the Smith family returned to the East. During the years 1838–43, Smith's father served as the pastor of the Presbyterian church on West Second Street in Frederick. He also functioned as the headmaster of a local school. That seems to have been a custom during that time period, as many pastors served in that dual capacity.

Young Smith entered Union Seminary as a divinity student in Farmville in 1860. He watched the local militia drilling and heard the fiery speeches about the upcoming election.

Then came April 1861, and Virginia withdrew from the Union. James Smith, like a host of other young men, was faced with a dilemma. He was opposed to slavery and had doubts about secession. But he was a Virginian and believed in states' rights. Smith deferred as long as he could. Then he returned to Winchester and noted that young men were joining the ranks. Smith made up his mind and entered a camp north of town. There he reported to Captain William Nelson Pendleton of the Rockbridge Artillery.

From the camp south of Frederick, Smith rode into town and went to visit the church of his childhood. Going up to the balcony, he reflected on earlier days when his mother held him safe and secure in her arms. Leaving the church, he found that a horse thief had been at work—he had to walk back to camp.

Upon his arrival, he was told to report to General Jackson. He thought that his comrades were playing a trick on him. Being reassured that the general really did want to see him, Smith made his way to the general's tent. The young minister's son had caught the eye of Stonewall. Smith was asked to be a staff member.

Smith quickly made friends with Douglas and Pendleton. There was a common thread in their lives. The three were ministers' sons. The three, along with Dr. Hunter McGuire, spent the winter of 1862–63 together at Moss Neck Manor near Fredericksburg. There they took care of the administrative details of Jackson's command.

Smith was nearby when Lee and Jackson had their famed "cracker box" conference on the eve of the Chancellorsville campaign. It was at this time that the two famed generals planned Jackson's flank march with routed O.O. Howard's Eleventh Corps. His description of that moment remains a gem for Civil War students.

Smith arrived on the scene shortly after Jackson was mortally wounded on the evening of May 2. Along with Douglas and Pendleton, he accompanied Jackson's body to Richmond and then to Lexington. He wrote extensively on his commander's death and burial.

During the Gettysburg campaign, Smith served as a courier for R.S. Ewell and also for Robert E. Lee. He lamented Douglas's serious wound. In 1864, he crossed the Potomac with Jubal Early and was with that command during the ransom of Frederick and Battle of Monocacy. Smith came through the war unscratched physically but carried with him the trauma of the sights and sounds of combat.

With the cessation of hostilities, Smith assumed the pastorate of a Presbyterian church near Roanoke. Then came the invitation to become pastor of the Presbyterian church in Fredericksburg. He was installed in November 1869 and remained in that pastorate for the next twenty-three years.

High on a hill on the east bank of the Rappahannock at Fredericksburg is Chatham. Construction on the mansion was begun in 1768 by William Fitzhugh. Tradition has it that George and Martha Washington spent part of their honeymoon at Chatham. Lincoln came to the mansion in the spring of 1862 to discuss strategy with his generals.

In 1870, Chatham was owned by the Lacy family. Young Pastor Smith came courting the daughter of Horace and Betty Lacy. The young couple was married at Chatham on April 26, 1871. Years later, one of their descendants married into the family of the esteemed cleric Norman Vincent Peale.

Smith was a busy man. Not only did he build up the Presbyterian church, he also became editor of a church newspaper and served as clerk or secretary of the Virginia Synod of the Presbyterian Church for fifty years.

Smith also assisted Confederate veterans, both spiritually and economically. He attended gatherings of the United Confederate Veterans and conducted services for his comrades in gray as they answered "the last roll call."

The nation was fascinated by the life of Jackson. As time took its toll on those who knew the famed general, Smith was in demand for speeches and articles. He was a prolific writer and wrote for both Northern and Southern periodicals and books, including the Century Company, which later compiled the collection of writings into a four-volume set called *Battles and Leaders of the Civil War.*

Once asked about Jackson, Smith said, "When the Lord decided it was time for the South to lose the war, he took General Jackson from our midst."

As a chaplain in the United Confederate Veterans, Smith gave the invocation at the dedication of the monument to Dr. Hunter Holmes McGuire in Richmond in January 1904, as well as the dedication to the Jackson Memorial at the Virginia Military Institute. Smith then returned to Gettysburg on June 9, 1917, to offer the prayer at the dedication of the Virginia State Monument on Seminary Ridge.

Smith, known and loved by all, died on August 6, 1923. Chatham, the estate where he courted his wife, is now headquarters of the Fredericksburg

National Military Park. Child psychologists say that the first years of life are formative. James Power Smith spent his first years in Frederick.

William Nelson Pendleton came from one of Virginia's first families. He graduated from West Point and fulfilled his military obligations. Then Pendleton entered the Episcopal priesthood and became the rector of All Saints Episcopal Church in Frederick. He served in that capacity from 1846 to 1854. He also rode to Catoctin Furnace, helping that parish in time of need.[2]

The senior Pendleton desired to erect a new sanctuary in Frederick. There were several reasons. Nearby were three livery stables, and in the summer without the benefit of modern air conditioning, the smells and flies were somewhat obnoxious. The new building did not materialize, so Pendleton accepted the call to a church in Lexington, Virginia. There Pendleton served the rest of his life. Prior to the beginning of the Civil War, Pendleton had trained the Lexington Artillery unit, later to become the famous Rockbridge Artillery. He served during the war as an artillery officer in the Army of Northern Virginia. In appearance and demeanor, he reminded people of Robert E. Lee.

Pendleton conducted Robert E. Lee's funeral service. After the war, residents of Frederick sent care packages to their former pastor and family in Lexington.[3]

A son, Alexander Swift "Sandie" Pendleton, was born on September 28, 1840. Small in stature, Sandie was often picked on by bullies in Frederick. His mother told him to stand up for himself. After the move to Lexington, Sandie attended Washington College, now Washington and Lee University. On the outbreak of the war, he hastened to Harpers Ferry with Virginia militia units.

In time, Sandie became almost like a son to Jackson. Both were very religious. In the ranks, there was a question, "Who prays more, Jackson or Pendleton?" Sandie often stated that when the war was over, he hoped to become an Episcopal priest.

After the Battle of Fredericksburg, Jackson's command went into winter quarters at Moss Neck Manor. There Pendleton fell in love with Catherine "Kate" Corbin. Due to the war, their marriage had to be postponed until December 1863. Henry Kyd Douglas was one of the groomsmen.

During the previous winter, Douglas, Pendleton and Dr. Hunter Holmes McGuire, the brigade surgeon, shared a tent, often reading from Shakespeare and other literary works.

Sandie was in Frederick in July 1864 when Jubal Early levied a ransom on Frederick. He and his friends took a break from military activities and obtained some ice cream.

In September 1864, Sandie was seeking to rally retreating Confederate forces at Fisher's Hill. He was mortally wounded and died a few days later in Woodstock. On November 4, Kate brought forth a little boy. Of course, like many others, the baby entered the world without a father.

Pendleton is buried at the cemetery at the south end of Lexington, Virginia, near his parents and his beloved commander, Thomas J. Jackson. In Confederate ranks, Pendleton was considered by many to be the finest staff officer in the Army of Northern Virginia. This staff officer and preacher's son spent his early days in Frederick.

Robert Douglas moved to the United States from Scotland and entered the ministry of the German Reformed Church. His first parish was in Shepherdstown, Virginia. While serving in Shepherdstown, he and his wife had a son. They named him Henry Kyd.

Henry's mother died, and Reverend Douglas married Miss Helen Blackford, the daughter of one of Shepherdstown's prominent citizens. Mr. Blackford not only owned and operated Ferry Hill Plantation just across the Potomac River in Maryland. He also operated Blackford's Ferry. The famous Pack Hose Ford is also sometimes known as Blackford's Ford.[4]

Henry attended a German reformed college, Franklin and Marshall in Lancaster. He kept a wonderful journal of college life and summers at Ferry Hill. Upon graduation, Henry entered the legal field.

In 1861, Henry hastened to Harpers Ferry. He enlisted in Company B, Second Virginia Infantry. There five Virginia regiments were honed into an outstanding military unit by an officer from the Virginia Military Institute by the name of Thomas J. Jackson.

Douglas was with the brigade when the immortal words were uttered by General Bee: "There stands Jackson like a stone wall! Rally behind the Virginians!"

We are indebted to Douglas for giving us the words of Jackson's famous speech to the First Brigade when he was assigned to command at Winchester.

Joyfully, the Brigade of Virginia regiments were assigned to Jackson. Douglas thus participated in the famed Shenandoah Valley campaign.

In the Maryland campaign, Henry's mother came to the bivouac area south of Frederick to visit her son and to meet Jackson. And it was Douglas who had arranged Jackson's passage into Frederick to attend services at German Reformed Church, served by a close family friend, Dr. Daniel Zacharias. It was Douglas who noted that Jackson never rode by Barbara Fritchie's house.

Douglas lamented his commander's death and, along with Pendleton and Smith, accompanied the body to Richmond and Lexington.

During the Gettysburg campaign, Douglas visited his Ferry Hill home as Confederate troops crossed at Blackford's Ford. The great Confederate cartographer Jed Hotchkiss worked on maps of Pennsylvania at Ferry Hill.

Douglas entered Pennsylvania with anger and revenge on his mind. After the Battle of Antietam, Union troops occupied Ferry Hill. On a windy night, a shutter blew open. A Union sentry saw it, and the officers were convinced that the Douglas family was signaling Confederate forces across the river.

Henry's father was imprisoned. He died five years after Antietam. Henry was convinced that the harsh imprisonment hastened his father's demise. Several outbuildings were burned. All that remained in 1863 were the blackened ruins.

Douglas almost lost his life on Culp's Hill at Gettysburg on July 2. While leading a brigade into action, a hail of bullets tore into his left shoulder. Douglas slumped forward on "Ashby's neck." A Union soldier rushed forward and took his sword.

The wound was ragged and serious. The ball carried part of Henry's coat into the body, as well as slivers from his shirt and undershirt. It lodged under the clavicle. He was taken to a house in Hunterstown, north of Gettysburg, and laid on the floor. Being seriously wounded, Douglas remained in a Union hospital for a month and was then taken to a large hospital in Baltimore.

On April 9, 1865, the ragged, tattered Army of Northern Virginia surrendered at Appomattox. Douglas was the last commander of the Stonewall Brigade, now numbering just a little more than two hundred. As his men had fired the last Confederate shots of the war,

Douglas requested that his men would be the last to stack arms. The request was granted.

Douglas left Appomattox on his horse, named Jeb Stuart, with his uniform and a fifty-cent Confederate note. En route home, he acquiesced to a photograph in Martinsburg in his uniform. That was forbidden. Hence, Douglas was arrested and imprisoned next to the Lincoln conspirators in Washington. He was an eyewitness to their deaths.

After his release, Douglas practiced law in Hagerstown, Maryland, and Winchester, Virginia. He was instrumental in the establishment of the Confederate cemeteries in Hagerstown and Shepherdstown. He presided over several Memorial Day programs at Antietam's National Cemetery and even hosted George B. McClellan when the general came to speak in 1884. Douglas also presided over the dedication of the Maryland Monument on May 30, 1900. Although he had served the Confederacy, he became adjutant general of the Maryland militia or National Guard.

Dr. Hunter Holmes McGuire, who signed the Frederick ransom note. *Virginia State Historical Society.*

As Douglas reflected on life in 1899, he noted that his hair as a young man was black and now was gray. Instead of keen eyesight, he now wore glasses. And many of his comrades of the 1860s had answered the last roll call.

During his last years, he wrote notes about his wartime years. These were added to his wartime journals and placed in a trunk. In the late 1930s, these materials were discovered by a nephew, John Kyd Beckenbaugh. They were submitted to the University of North Carolina Press and printed in 1940. After seventy years, the book remains in print. The original manuscripts of Henry Kyd Douglas are located at the Bast Museum in Boonsboro.

Chapter 8

ROADS TO AND FROM GETTYSBURG, 1863

The year 1863 brought the third year of the Lincoln presidency. The only bright spots thus far were the victory at Antietam and the Emancipation Proclamation.

Fredericksburg and then Burnside's infamous "Mud March" were Union disasters. Lincoln once again sought a man or a general for the moment. "Fighting Joe" Hooker, so named by correspondents, replaced Burnside. The Army of Northern Virginia and the Army of the Potomac remained in winter quarters, facing each other across the Rappahannock River.

The first three days of May brought Robert E. Lee's brilliant victory at Chancellorsville, west of Fredericksburg. Jackson made his famous flanking march and routed O.O. Howard's Eleventh Corps. Hooker was stunned by the brilliance of Jackson's attack and once again retreated.

However, in the success at Chancellorsville, the South, according to some, may have lost the war. On the evening of May 2, while riding near the front, mighty Stonewall went down in a hail of bullets fired mistakenly by his own troops.

After his arm was amputated, Jackson was taken to Guiney Station. He seemed on the road to recovery when he was stricken with pneumonia (and perhaps an embolism). Thus, on Sunday, May 10, Jackson uttered the words, "Let us cross over the river and rest in the shade of the trees." He was irreplaceable. Earlier, Lee had written, "You have lost your left arm, but I have lost my right arm."

Half of the great military team of Lee and Jackson was gone. Together, the generals in gray had operated in tandem. Now Lee was forced to reorganize the Army of Northern Virginia. James Longstreet was retained as commander of the First Corps, while Jackson's command was divided between Richard Ewell and Ambrose P. Hill.

For Lee and the Confederacy, it was time to take the initiative again. It was approaching summertime, and it was the summertime of the Confederacy as well. If it was ever going to reap a victory, now was the hour to strike.

After the Battle of Chancellorsville, the Army of Northern Virginia was brimming with confidence. It had unbounded confidence in its esteemed leader, Robert E. Lee.

On June 3, Lee began to disengage from his line along near Fredericksburg and along the south bank of the Rappahannock River. Lee entered the campaign with new commanders, but he began his march from the banks of the Rappahannock to the very gates of Harrisburg and the fields of Gettysburg.

Ewell moved with rapidity and momentarily reminded some of another Jackson. On June 14 and 15, Ewell's corps swept aside the troops of Nathaniel Banks at Winchester. It was a huge Southern victory. The next day, the command of Robert Rodes crossed the Potomac at Williamsport. Elements of Alfred's Jenkins cavalry proceeded northward to Greencastle and into Franklin County, Pennsylvania. They helped themselves to cattle, sheep and hogs, sending them back to Virginia. Then Lee and the rest of the Army of Northern Virginia crossed the Potomac at Shepherdstown and Williamsport. By June 27, Confederate troops were encamped around Chambersburg, ready to push on to Carlisle and Harrisburg. There was great alarm in Pennsylvania, as well as in central Maryland. Joe Hooker and the Army of the Potomac were in a quandary. They did not know where Lee was or what he was up to. Lee had stolen a march on the Union commander.

We are all familiar with Gettysburg. However, the movement of about 200,000 troops, and all the implements of war, is an epic story. More than fifty thousand horses and mules pulled the supply wagons, cannons, caissons and ambulances. The story of Gettysburg begins on the banks of the Rappahannock—for some in the Army of Northern Virginia, it was 250 miles on foot. A West Point graduate says that if the Union army would have been lined up according to military protocol, the line would have been eighty-four miles long.

Roads to Gettysburg involved the creaking of wagons, the rumbling of the wheels, the braying of donkeys, heat, clouds of dust, extreme thirst and, in some cases, death by heat exhaustion. For the Army of the Potomac, the route led through Frederick County and to Frederick City, the crossroads of the Civil War.

Hooker faced a major hurdle: crossing the Potomac River. In a great feat, the engineers of the army laid a pontoon bridge from the Virginia shore near Leesburg to Edward's Ferry in Maryland, near Poolesville. Boats held the wooden planking. During the days of June 24–27, about 100,000 troops crossed the Potomac River on two bridges. Most of the time it rained. At that moment, it was the greatest river crossing ever achieved in America. Later in the war, more men would cross at the James River.

With Sugar Loaf Mountain rising majestically to the east, the left wing of the Union army, commanded by John Fulton Reynolds, marched via Barnesville, Mountville and Jefferson into the fertile Middletown Valley. The First, Third and Eleventh Corps were entrusted with protecting the passes in the South Mountain range, preventing Lee from moving eastward on Washington. The Union soldiers were impressed with the lush pastures, sleek cattle and huge "Dutch barns." They noted the "beautiful fields of golden grain almost ready for the reaper as well as the well laden cherry trees."

As the Army of the Potomac approached Frederick, they paused to bathe and wash their clothing in the refreshing waters of the Monocacy River and Catoctin Creek.

By Saturday evening, squadrons of Union cavalry were encamping at Richfield, just north of Frederick, while Union artillery was being parked at Rose Hill Manor. Union infantry were approaching the city, and Joe Hooker established his headquarters on a commanding hill overlooking the city of Frederick.

Jacob Engelbrecht writes that the streets were "full of wagons and cavalry and infantry." Union soldiers who had survived Antietam, Fredericksburg and Chancellorsville remembered the great reception they received en route to Antietam Creek. Those who could were preparing to go into Frederick for a night on the town. There would be "a hot time" in Frederick.

Meanwhile, a big decision had been made in Washington. "Fighting Joe" Hooker had to go. None other than President Lincoln made the decision, with concurrence by Secretary of War Stanton. Earlier, John Fulton Reynolds had refused the offer of command. Now Lincoln and Stanton turned to another Pennsylvanian by the name of George Gordon Meade.

The orders were drawn up, a copy for Hooker and another for Meade. General Henry Halleck in the War Department was ordered to send a letter to Meade freeing him to act according to the need of the situation.

The officer selected to carry the orders to Frederick was carefully chosen. The messenger was Colonel James A. Hardie, Stanton's chief of staff, a West Point graduate. Hardie, after service on the frontier, had returned to the academy as an instructor. He had also been on McClellan's staff. Hardie was a highly respected and trusted officer. It was hoped that Hardie, being a personal friend of both Meade and Hooker, would make a difficult situation a little easier. Dressing in civilian clothing, Hardie, acting as the personal representative of the United States, boarded the train for Frederick.

While all of this was happening, Meade and the Fifth Corps had made their way to Arcadia on the Buckeystown Pike, near Ballenger Creek. Arcadia was a fine country estate owned by Robert McGill. In the early years of the 1800s, the farm was owned by Arthur Shaff, a brother-in-law of both Roger Brooke Taney and Robert Francis Scott Key. Both lawyers were frequent visitors to the farm.

West of Frederick, in Middletown Valley, Rufus Dawes, accompanied by some friends, climbed the slopes of South Mountain, there they paused to remember some of their comrades who had given their "last full measure of devotion" during the action on September 14, 1862. Thick grass now covered the graves, and they were hard to locate.

As evening came and the farmers finished their chores, many came to visit the camps of the men in blue. They brought their children to share the experience of a lifetime, and in Frederick, men in blue were descending on the taverns in droves.

The men in blue had endured long marches, soaking rains and extreme heat and thirst. They were due some rest and relaxation. They found it in Frederick. Just as September 13, 1862, would live in the memory of the veterans, so would Saturday, June 27. Despite orders to the contrary, guards winked as the troops slipped into the city, where they made merry with the townsfolk, ate at hotel tables and drank at hotel bars. Some say that the Army of the Potomac consumed more liquor on this night than any other night in the war. Many were late getting back to camp, and there were many hangovers.

While the troops of the Army of the Potomac were having a great night with good food and drink in Fredericktown, intrigue was afoot. Not only was a train bringing Colonel Hardie to Frederick with a message for George G. Meade, but a man by the name of Harrison was also mingling with the troops and moving around the campgrounds. He was a Confederate spy hired by James Longstreet as a special agent. He learned that the Army of the Potomac was heading for Pennsylvania.[1]

George Gordon Meade had led the Fifth Corps of the Army of the Potomac across the river to Arcadia, south of Frederick. He went to bed as the commander of an army corps. However, his military life was about to change dramatically.

Meade was born in Cadiz, Spain, in 1815. His father died prior to George reaching his teenage years. He was placed in a boarding school in Philadelphia. His mentor was Salmon P. Chase, later secretary of the U.S. Treasury. Graduating from West Point, he was assigned to the Third Artillery. Resigning from the army, he went into civil engineering but reentered the army during the Mexican-American War. In 1861, Meade was commissioned a brigadier general of volunteers and commanded a brigade and then a division of Pennsylvania troops. He marched through Frederick in September 1862 in command of a division that saw action in the cornfield at Antietam. Then he became a corps commander.

The clock of Trinity Chapel in Frederick struck two and then three. Would he never make it? Finally sometime after 3:00 a.m. on Sunday, June 28, Colonel Hardie reached Meade's tent. But now he faced another problem. The guard was not about to let Meade be wakened. However, Hardie prevailed.

Meade was dumbfounded. His first thought was that he was under arrest. But he could not imagine the charge. When Hardie told him that he had come as a representative of Mr. Lincoln with an order to assume command of the army, Meade was distressed. It was not right. The command should go to Reynolds. In fact, he insisted, saying that such an order was an injustice to his good friend John Reynolds. Besides, he didn't even know the location of the commands of the Army of the Potomac, let alone the Confederates. Meade argued further that he should not go to Hooker's tent to assume command. His superior should send for him. But Hardie said, "You no longer have a superior here. You are in command of the army."[2]

Meade had no recourse but to obey. Horses were prepared and an escort obtained. And in the early morning hours of the Sabbath, several horsemen went to Hooker's headquarters. One look told Hooker what was coming. Hardie broke the news. It was a trying and tense time. Meade, Hardie, Hooker and his chief of staff, Daniel Butterfield, sat down and went over the maps and other items necessary for the transfer of command.

Charles C. Coffin of the *Boston Globe* was at army headquarters when the command changed:

> *He* [Meade] *was standing with bowed head and downcast eyes, his slouched hat drawn down, shading his features. He seemed lost in thought…there was dust upon his boots. As a faithful soldier, loyal to duty, he accepted the great responsibility which had been thrust upon him.*
>
> *While General Hooker, shaking hands with him and with his officers, with tears coursing down his cheeks, bade them farewell.*[3]
>
> [Meade wrote:] *"It has pleased Almighty God to place me in the trying position that we have been talking about…At 3:00 a.m., I was aroused from my sleep by an officer from Washington entering my tent, and after waking me up, saying he had come to give me trouble. At first I thought that it was either to relieve or arrest me, and promptly replied to him, that my conscience was clear, void of offense towards any man; I was prepared for his bad news. He then handed me a communication to read; which I found was an order relieving Hooker from the command and assigning me to it…As a soldier, I had nothing to do but accept and exert my utmost abilities command success. This, so help me God, I will do, and trusting to Him, who in His good pleasure has thought it proper to place me where I am, I shall pray for strength and power to get through the task assigned me…I am moving at once against Lee, whom I am in hopes Couch will at least check for a few days; if so, a battle will decide the fate of our country and our cause. Pray earnestly, pray for the success of my country."*[4]

Pleasonton and the cavalry, or part of it, was at the north end of Harmony Grove along the Emmitsburg Road. General Tyler and the artillery reserve were one mile north of Frederick, probably on the grounds of Rose Hill Manor and what is now Governor Thomas Johnson High School. John Reynolds and the First Corps were at Middletown, with part of the First Division near Mount Tabor Church. The Second Corps under Hancock was on the way from Sugar Loaf Mountain to Monocacy Junction. The Third Corps was at Middletown. The Fifth was south of Frederick along the Buckeystown Road, the Sixth was near Barnesville, the Eleventh was in the Middletown Valley and the Twelfth was on the road from Knoxville to Fredericktown.

Church bells were ringing north of the Mason-Dixon line. However, residents of Chambersburg, Carlisle and York were slow to go to their houses of worship. Confederate troops were in their midst. The stars and stripes had been pulled from the flagpoles. Southern flags fluttered in the June breeze.

Meanwhile, church bells were also pealing in the village of Burkittsville, located about fifteen miles west of Frederick. Elements of the Union Third Corps struck camp and began their trek to Frederick. Soldiers in the New England units were reminded of home and loved ones far away en route to church in their hometowns. The bells reminded the lads of better days, as well as the profound hope that someday soon they would return to their beloved homes.

During the last Sabbath in June, the officer corps of the Army of the Potomac paid their respects to the new commander. Among them were John Reynolds, Winfield Scott Hancock and John Gibbon. Reynolds was happy with the decision.

John Reynolds was gracious and warm, a truly great man. He said, "The command has fallen where it belongs. I am glad that the burden and responsibility did not fall on me. You can count on my earnest support."

Meade knew that the enemy was out there and that a major battle was looming. Shortly after the change of command, Meade issued an order:

By direction of the President of the United States, I hereby assume command of The Army of the Potomac...as a soldier obeying this order, an order that came unexpected and unsolicited, I have no promises or pledges to make.

*The country looks to this army to relieve it from the devastation and
disgrace of a foreign invasion…let each man determine to do his duty,
leaving to an all controlling providence the direction of the contest.*

In accordance with the wishes of Alfred Pleasonton, the cavalry
commander of the Army of the Potomac, Meade signed an order
promoting three young captains to the rank of brigadier general. Senior
officers were bypassed. Welsey Merritt was one of the young officers. He
had risen in rank and commanded the U.S. Army during the Spanish-
American War. A military installation is named for him. He was wounded
during cavalry fighting at Fairfield, Pennsylvania. Elon Farnsworth,
a captain in the Eighth Illinois Cavalry, did not have long to enjoy his
promotion. He was killed at Gettysburg. The third young officer was just
twenty-three years of age. He had obtained a hotel room in Frederick
and was informed of his promotion. He had a big ego and wanted to look
the part of a general. He went to a tailor and obtained a velvet jacket
with gold braid. The next day, he assumed command of a brigade of
cavalry. The officer was none other than George Armstrong Custer. The
boy general began his rise to fame in Frederick.[5]

Charles C. Coffin, war correspondent.
U.S. Military History Institute.

Most of the officers and men in the Army of the Potomac respected George G. Meade. Theodore Gerrish, a member of the Twentieth Maine, wrote:

> *It was the most critical moment in the history of our country. General Lee, with a veteran army...flushed with victory, was on Northern soil; behind him was a desperate South, determined to make his campaign successful. Our foreign relations were in a critical condition. England and France were both in active sympathy with the South, and were only awaiting a decisive rebel victory to acknowledge the Confederacy as a nation, and then raise the blockade. A portion of the people had been opposed to the war from the beginning, and our repeated defeats had strengthened their opposition. Some feared that Lee would be able to dictate peace terms.*[6]

Unsure of the location of Lee's army, and not knowing what to expect from the general known as "the Gray Fox," Meade prepared for any possible attacks from Confederate infantry and/or cavalry. He made troops depositions "for guarding the approaches to Frederick against any possible dash of cavalry."

He assigned the troops new locations as follows:

> *From Moncocacy Junction to the bridge above Carroll Creek, near L.M. Thomas' Second Corps.*
> *From Thomas' to George Schultz's, on the road to Hamburg, Eleventh Corps.*
> *From (Schultz's) to the Middletown Road, near D.R. Miller's, First Corps.*
> *From (Miller's) to Zimmerman's, on the Ballenger Creek, Twelfth Corps.*
> *From (Zimmerman's), to connect with the Second Corps, by Ballenger Creek and the Monocacy, Fifth Corps.*[7]

The corps commanders were instructed to carefully guard their trains and camps on marches and halts. Staff officers of each corps were instructed to bring morning and evening reports. All units were instructed to be ready to move at daylight. Headquarters would move out at 8:00 a.m.

No time was to be lost. Indeed, time was of the essence. Meade therefore had the following order delivered to the army:

Headquarters Army of the Potomac
Frederick, Md.
June 28, 1863

The army will march tomorrow as follows:
4 a.m. The 1st Corps, Major General Reynolds by Lewistown and Mechanicstown to Emmetsburg, keeping to the left of the road from Frederick to Lewistown, between J.P. Cramer's and where the road branches to Utica and Creagerstown, to enable the 11th Corps to march parallel to it.

4 a.m. The 11th Corps, Major General Howard, by Utica and Creagerstown to Emmetsburg.

4 a.m. The 12th Corps, by Ceresville, Walkersville and Woods-borough to Taney town.

4 a.m. The 3rd Corps by Woodsborough and Middleburg [from Walkersville], *to Taneytown.*

4 a.m. The 2nd Corps, by Johnsville, Liberty and Union, to Frizzleburg.

The Engineers and bridge-trains will follow the 5th Corps. Headquarters will move at 8 a.m. and be tomorrow night at Middleburg. Headquarters' train will move by Ceresville and Woodsborough to Middleburg, at 8 a.m.

The Cavalry will guard the left and right flanks and the rear, and give the Commanding General information of the movement and of the enemy in front.

Corps commanders and commanders of detached brigades will report by staff officer their positions tomorrow night and on all marches in future.[8]

By midafternoon, the leading elements of the Union Third Corps reached Frederick. They had departed Burkittsville while the church bells were ringing. Their route was to Middletown and then east across Catoctin Mountain to the western part of Frederick to North Market Street. Edward Houghton wrote:

> *Frederick is a beautiful city, and was, judging from our reception, thoroughly Union in sentiment...from nearly every house the stars and stripes floated in the breeze...and the windows, housetops, and doorways were lined with ladies in their holiday attire waving their handkerchiefs and American flags. We marched nearly a mile through the streets of the city and our progress was one continuous ovation. Nothing since our military career commenced equaled the enthusiasm we received here. The day, the occasion, and the reception we received, will be forever cherished in the members of the soldiers in the Third Corps.*[9]

Regis DeTrobriand was an officer in the Third Corps. Somewhere in Frederick, his column was hailed by a throng of admirers. A little girl was given a bouquet of flowers by her mother. She made her way through the crowd and held the flowers up to the general. He leaned forward in the saddle and graciously received the tokens of admiration. The lass said, "Good luck, General." The officer wanted to dismount and hug the little girl. However, there was no time, but as he rode away, DeTrobriand turned in the saddle and blew her a kiss.[10]

Colonel Schoonover noted that men and women brought buckets of water and dippers to the thirsty soldiers. They drank as they marched by, much like runners taking fluids in marathon races. Ladies also brought baskets of sandwiches.[11]

The march continued to Ceresville and a bivouac in the fields near Walkersville. Tomorrow the march would continue on what is Route 194 to Taneytown and the Peach Orchard at Gettysburg.

In Frederick, the Third Corps was reunited with its commander, Dan Sickles. He had been in Washington. Sickles was the first man to be tried for murder and deemed not guilty by pleading temporary insanity. On July 1, Sickles lost his leg at Gettysburg.

Entering Frederick from the southwest, from campgrounds near Prospect Hall and the Harpers Ferry Road, was Henry Warner Slocum and the Twelfth Corps. Henry was born in New York on September 24, 1827. He was also a West Point graduate. Following graduation, he had tours of duty at Charleston Harbor and in action against the Seminoles. Slocum resigned from the army in 1856 and moved to Syracuse. There he practiced law, became the county treasurer and then served in the state legislature. Upon the outbreak of hostilities, Slocum became colonel of the Twenty-seventh New York. At First Bull Run, the regiment suffered heavy losses, and Slocum was wounded. At the age of thirty-four, he was appointed a major general, and after the death of Joseph Mansfield at Antietam, he was promoted to command the Twelfth Corps.[12]

Catherine Reynolds and her sister lived on West Second Street. On Saturday, she walked a few steps to Market Street and inquired of some of the troops headed to Richfield if General Reynolds was near. They said no but that the infantry would be soon coming.

On Sunday, Catherine waited for "Cousin John," not just a general but also a relative. During the wait, the Reynolds girls fed seventeen hungry Union soldiers and gave bread to many others. Catherine gave no thought as to what her neighbors, Southern sympathizers, might have thought.

Major General George G. Meade.
Library of Congress.

As the shades of night fell, Catherine gave up any hope of seeing "Cousin John." But a little after 9:00 p.m. there was a knock at the door, and there he was. He sat at the table and seemed to enjoy the meal of cold roast beef, yellow pickles and cherry pie.[13]

General Reynolds had ridden ahead of his command to pay his respects to the new commander of the Potomac, a fellow Pennsylvanian, George G. Meade. Three members of the general's staff remained in the saddle during his brief visit. Catherine prepared sandwiches for them as they rode back to headquarters.

Cousin John promised to return. Alas, it was the last time the girls would see their cousin. While leading his troops to save the day on July 1, he was shot in the head and killed west of Gettysburg.

Reynolds rode north and made his headquarters about a mile north of the city, perhaps at Rose Hill Manor. He would be in the center of his command, the Third Corps being in Walkersville, the First at the west end of Frederick and the Eleventh on the way.

Oliver O. Howard and his command did not get the reception accorded other units—it was nearly 9:30 p.m. when they reached Frederick. They continued marching in the darkness until they reached the junction of Baltimore-Emmitsburg Road at Worman's Mill, currently U.S. 15 and 26.

North of Frederick in Messersmith's Woods, west of Chambersburg, a rider approached the tent of James Longstreet; it was Harrison. He had experienced a harrowing ride through Union patrols. He carried the news that the Army of the Potomac was across the river and had a new commander. He was taken to Lee's tent.

The news was most disturbing. General Ewell was in sight of Harrisburg and Jubal Early in York. Now the army had to be recalled. The enemy was not far away. Peering at a map, General Lee pointed to the Cashtown-Gettysburg area. The army would regroup there.

Couriers were dispatched in the darkness. When Richard Ewell received the orders, he fumed and fussed. He was within sight of Harrisburg and would have to forego his attack. Likewise, Confederate troops at Carlisle and York were ordered to retrace their steps to a place called Gettysburg.

A light rain was falling on Monday morning during the day when the troops of both armies took long marches on the roads to Gettysburg.

In the Army of Northern Virginia, the angry R.S. Ewell headed south from the Susquehanna River toward Gettysburg and the rest of the army would also head for Gettysburg. Each command had about thirty miles to cover.

Howard's men at Worman's Mill had a short night. They were awakened at 3:45 a.m. and took the Old Frederick Road to Emmitsburg, followed by John Reynolds and the First Corps. The Third and Twelfth Corps and General Meade himself traveled from Frederick to Ceresville along what is now Route 194. The Second and Fifth Corps were to the east on Router 26 and the Gas House Pike. However, it is to be noted that the entire Army of the Potomac, with the exception of the Sixth Corps, marched through Frederick on the roads to Gettysburg. The Sixth Corps was entrusted with protecting the right flank of the Army of the Potomac.

The First Corps, 9,400 strong, entered Frederick during the early hours of Monday. Abner Doubleday, the supposed founder of baseball, commanded the First Division. He noted that "it was a miserable dreary day, long and toilsome."[14]

Riding proudly with Battery B, Fourth U.S. Artillery, was Lieutenant James Stewart. He had almost lost his horse, Old Tartar, at Chancellorsville—not to enemy fire but rather during a visit from President Lincoln. The horse had lost its tail at Manassas when a shell grazed both hips. Thus, Tartar was also known as the "horse without a tail."[15]

At about 8:00 a.m., Meade mounted Old Baldy at Prospect Hall. He followed the Twelfth Corps on a twenty-five-mile ride to Taneytown in Carroll County.

A.S. Williams of the Twelfth Corps was awakened at 2:30 a.m. There was a courier from Meade's headquarters ordering the command to be on the road to Taneytown by 5:30 a.m. Williams had made camp in a nice grove of trees and was reluctant to leave. His troops had been on the road since June 24 and were very tired. Stopping momentarily in Frederick at Dr. Steiner's office, he dashed off a note to his daughters, saying that he had been careful in his remarks about Joe Hooker but that he held him in utter contempt.[16]

In most camps, there was a problem with soldiers recovering from their Saturday night on the town. Some were just emerging from their stupors. Edmund Brown of the Twenty-seventh Indiana says that the rain helped him sober up. Brown was very fond of Frederick; this was his third visit to the city. It seemed almost like home to him and to many others. Meade issued

Prospect Hall. *Author's collection.*

an order addressing the situation: "The Major General commanding directs that you take immediate and prompt measures to have all the stragglers and drunken soldiers driven out of Frederick and sent to their commands."[17]

South of Frederick, on the banks of the Monocacy, Winfield Scott Hancock was fuming and fussing. It was almost 8:00 a.m. The army was supposed to move northward, and orders had not yet arrived. There had been a mix-up and poor communication from army headquarters. The orders finally arrived, and Hancock led the Second Corps into Frederick and struck the Gas House Pike. The corps had miles and miles to go before they slept—thirty-two in fact.

Hancock was born in Montgomery Square, Pennsylvania, on February 14, 1824, graduating from West Point twenty years later. Tours of duty on the plains and in California followed. He also marched through Frederick, in September 1862. Near the Sunken Road, later named Bloody Lane, Hancock replaced the fallen Israel B. Richardson as a division commander and then gained corps command. His command and control at Gettysburg are legendary. The troops marching through Frederick on June 29 repulsed Pickett's Charge on July 3; in that action Hancock was severely wounded.

On this rainy Monday, the Second Corps tramped through Liberty and Unionville and then to Uniontown in Carroll County. It covered thirty miles. Correspondent Charles C. Coffin rode with Hancock.

Joshua Lawrence Chamberlain, a member of the Fifth Corps, was impressed with the prosperity of the Frederick area as opposed to war-torn Virginia. He noted the towns of Mount Pleasant and Liberty. The former Bowdoin College professor was on the verge of military fame for his actions at Little Round Top on July 2.

While the infantry was plodding northward in the mist and rain, George Armstrong Custer, the newly promoted general, rode from Frederick to the Emmitsburg Pike to Richfield Farm. There he assumed command of a brigade of Michigan cavalry. Later, his battle cry became famous as: "Come on, you wolverines!" But on this day, the troopers looked on in amazement at their new commander, complete with a velvet jacket and gold braid.

For both armies, it had been a long and difficult day. The Union army had marched on five roads: the Emmitsburg Pike; the Old Frederick Road; the road to Taneytown; the Baltimore Road, now Route 29; and the National Road toward Baltimore. Troopers advanced eighteen to thirty-two miles, moving like the finger of a glove. They were now closer to Gettysburg, and on the morrow the blue and gray would resume their marches.

John F. Reynolds and the left wing of the Union army was at or near Emmitsburg, with the other corps to the east; Meade maintained his headquarters at Taneytown, near the center of his army. Meandering through Frederick and Carroll County is Pipe Creek. Meade formulated a plan to establish a strong defensive position on the south bank of the creek should the army be overwhelmed.

On June 30, all were mustered for pay. However, not all of the troops were paid. For this was the last day of June, and a big battle would not be far away. Many soldiers were thinking about a song: "Just before the battle, Mother, I am thinking of home and you." Some were writing letters by candlelight. Others pinned their names and the names of the next of kin to their undershirts.

There was a major cavalry action at Hanover between Kilpatrick's Union forces and those under Jeb Stuart. Twelve miles east, John Buford established headquarters in the Eagle Hotel, while his troopers and horse artillery trotted a mile or so to the west and went into position with their left flank resting on the Fairfield Road and the right north of the Chambersburg Road. Buford's task: "Hold until the infantry arrived."

Buford's pickets found a warm night on Willoughby Run. John Buford climbed to the cupola of the Lutheran seminary. To the west, he could see campfires. They belonged to the infantry of A.P. Hill's Third Corps. The general spent an uneasy night. He knew that in the morning, he would be in the crossfire of the men in gray.

George Meade had assumed command of the Army of the Potomac in Frederick. Forty-eight hours later, his army engaged in a battle to determine the fate of the nation.

Daybreak found John Buford just west of Gettysburg on McPherson's Ridge. His troopers were prepared to fight as infantry. The cavalry were arranged in groups of four; three fought as infantry, while the fourth held the reins of the horses. Some say that this arrangement led to the mechanized cavalry of World War II.

At first light, Buford scanned the horizon. What he saw was alarming. To the west, there was the gleam of bayonets, red and blue banners and a mass of men in gray. Worse yet, they were headed right for him.

Quickly, couriers were sent east and south. One rode to convey the news of the approaching Confederates to General Meade at army headquarters in Taneytown, while another was sent to General Reynolds at Moritz Tavern eight miles away. Buford was requesting infantry support. Buford said that he would do his best to hold until reinforcements arrived.

The men of the First Corps—who had entered Frederick via the rough narrow Shookstown Pass on Sunday—were issued additional cartridges even as the chaplains were praying.

Crossing Marsh Creek, the fife and drum corps struck up a tune, "The Camp Bells Are Coming." Climbing the northern hill was the First Brigade of the First Division of the First Corps. It was an awesome sight. Soon it would be no more. The First Corps joined the cavalry and fought for dear life west of Gettysburg. However, it suffered horrendous casualties. And in the midst of it all, John Reynolds was killed.

Meanwhile, men were tramping through the dust and summer heat. Both armies were rushing additional troops to Gettysburg. Meade sent General Hancock from Taneytown to take control of the situation. Eventually, the Union line formed in the shape of a fishhook on Cemetery Ridge.

Some feel that the Confederates missed a golden opportunity to win a major victory by not exploiting the situation on July 1. Late in the day on July 2, the Confederates struck both flanks of the Union army. There was fighting at Little Round Top, in the Wheat Field and Peach Orchard at Culp's Hill and Cemetery Hill.

On July 3, two cannons boomed at 1:00 p.m. from Seminary Ridge. They signaled a barrage; the artillery of the Army of Northern Virginia spewed forth death and destruction, shelling Union lines a mile away.

Then, at three o'clock in the afternoon, a long line of butternut and gray emerged from the cover of the woods on Seminary Ridge. Previously, Lee had struck at the flanks of the Army of the Potomac; now he was assaulting the Union center with fifteen thousand troops in the event known as Pickett's Charge. The Rebel tide moved forward, crested and then receded. More than one-third of the attacking column was killed, wounded or ended up missing, including irreplaceable men of high caliber. Lee sadly met the retreating troops and said, "You have done your best. It's all my fault."

That night, Lee rode along Seminary Ridge alone in the moonlight, pondering his choices. Some say that this was Lee's Gethsemane. He had lost twenty-eight thousand men. Returning to headquarters, he met with Colonel John Imboden. He had a task for Imboden: arrange a wagon train and get the wounded back to Virginia.

As a result of Lee's decision, Frederick would once again hear the *tramp-tramp* of marching feet, as well as the rumble of the wagons and cannons of war, as Meade would disengage and follow Lee, keeping between the retreating Confederates army and Washington.

Saturday, July 4, was sultry. Then, late in the day, the heavens opened and a heavy rain descended on the armies at Gettysburg. Waters rose rapidly, and soldiers placed near streams had to be taken to higher ground. It was as though the tears of heaven were falling to cleanse the blood-soaked fields of Gettysburg.

At about 4:00 p.m. there was another rumble, barely audible above the falling rain. On Seminary Ridge, John Imboden was leaving Gettysburg with a seventeen-mile wagon train of wounded. Later to be known as the "Wagon train of misery," it was headed for Cashtown Pass. Shortly thereafter, Ewell's wagon train and then the Confederate infantry took the roads from Gettysburg, headed for Monterey Pass, Hagerstown and the Potomac.

John Buford's cavalry had opened the fighting at Gettysburg. Knowing that his men and mounts were tired, Buford sought Meade's permission to retire from the field for refitting purposes. Thus, he rode to Taneytown on July 2. It was a four-hour trip for the mounted column. Then it was on to Westminster, the Union base, thirty miles from Gettysburg. There Buford's men found rest and forage. Part of July 4 was spent in reshoeing the horses. Meade, anticipating Lee's withdrawal from Gettysburg, ordered Buford's men to "mount up," proceed to Frederick, cross the mountains and endeavor to cut off Lee's retreat. "Boots and saddles" was sounded just about the time the rain began. The troopers mounted up. The rain fell in torrents, and Buford, realizing that the night was neither fit for "man or beast," ordered a halt and bivouac.

Judson Kilpatrick and George Custer were also riding in the rain. They turned west in Emmitsburg and assailed Ewell's wagon train in Monterey Pass, capturing and destroying many of the wagons and taking nearly one thousand prisoners. They were escorted to Hagerstown and then to Frederick.

The next day, Meade sent John Sedgwick forward to conduct a reconnaissance in force. It was determined that the enemy was gone. Meade has been criticized for not following Lee in an aggressive manner. However, Meade had lost twenty-three thousand men, or almost one-fourth of his command. John Reynolds was dead. Winfield Scott Hancock and Dan Sickles were severely wounded. It would be hard to deploy infantry in the mountain passes against Lee.

Therefore, orders were given to retrace the roads to Gettysburg. The routes again led to Frederick, the crossroads of the Civil War. From Frederick, Meade could cross South Mountain at Turner's, Fox's and Crampton's Gaps and intercept Lee. The roads were bad, but it was hoped that rising waters would prevent Lee from crossing before Meade could strike. The supply base for the army had been located at Westminster. Now he would move it to Emmitsburg and, when the army reached Frederick, set up a supply depot at Monocacy Junction.

While the fighting raged at Gettysburg, a division commanded by William T. French occupied Frederick, a sort of rear guard in the event of a Federal disaster in Pennsylvania. Early on July 4, Meade ordered French to maintain his position and seize the South Mountain passes. French was also ordered to reoccupy the South Mountain passes if possible and harass Confederate lines of communication.

The weather was a little better on Sunday, July 5. Buford and his mud-splattered horses and men rode into Frederick and received cheers. Being late in the day, the troopers went into camp west of Frederick, presumably in the area of the Golden Mile. There they were joined by a portion of Wesley Merritt's command arriving from Mechanicstown or Thurmont. Buford pondered his orders to move to Williamsport and Falling Waters to prevent Lee's escape. General French had also brought some forage for Buford's horses.

In Frederick, some of Buford's men spotted a suspicious-looking character. They took him in for questioning. He claimed to be a Northern reporter. However, in his boot were papers indicating that he was a Confederate spy. His name was Richardson. When asked what to do, Buford said, "Hang him." Thus, he was strung up, and three troopers watched his death by hanging. His body was left swaying as a reminder to anyone who had notions of spying for the South.[18]

At Gettysburg, some of the Union infantry began their movements on the roads from Gettysburg. At dawn, on July 6, Buford led his 2,500 man force and two six-gun batteries from Frederick in pursuit of R.E. Lee. Thirteen hours were spent in saddle. During the next four days, Buford and his men would fight at Boonsboro, Beaver Creek, Williamsport and Funkstown. At the last place, Buford was almost killed when bullets passed through the sleeve of his jacket.

On Tuesday, July 7, Lincoln and the cabinet met to discuss the available news from Gettysburg. Lincoln, perhaps not realizing the ferocity of the battle and the condition of the men and horses, felt that Meade should have been at Hagerstown. That, of course, was impossible.

While the cabinet meeting was in progress, George Meade was riding south from Emmitsburg on the Old Frederick Road to Cregarstown and Utica to free Fredericktown.

George G. Meade reached Frederick late in the day. He found Frederick in a festive mood. Entering the city on North Market Street, he saw hundreds of flags lining the route, and cheers and shouts of joy greeted the general and his staff, as well as any man who wore the uniform of the Union. Everybody wanted to see the men who had stemmed the tide at Gettysburg, the troops who had defeated the famed Robert E. Lee. It was a day of rejoicing in Frederick.

There were several leading hotels in Frederick. Meade selected the U.S. Hotel at the southwest corner of South Market and All Saints Streets as his temporary headquarters. Part of the reason for the selection was the fact that the Baltimore & Ohio railroad station was located just across the street and was convenient for messengers, as well as telegraph couriers.

Once in the hotel, Meade began mapping a strategy to confront Lee west of the mountains. After marching and fighting for ten days, he implored the government to send him fresh supplies to replenish those used at Gettysburg. He was momentarily interrupted by a group of ladies from Frederick, who presented him with floral wreaths and bouquets. Meade felt that the Lincoln administration did not appreciate his efforts. Writing to his family, Meade said, "The people in this place have made a great fuss over me."

The people of Frederick found the victor of Gettysburg to be a quiet, unassuming, no-nonsense type of person. When he entered the hotel, his boots and lower trousers were splattered with mud. In many ways, he was much like Stonewall Jackson. He was uncomfortable with praise and adulation. Although Meade was just forty-seven years of age, he looked much older. He was partially balding and had a full gray beard. He wore a slouched hat. He did not care for military pomp. Some who had seen Meade at Prospect Hall on June 28 thought that he had aged ten years in ten days.

During the evening hours, a large crowd gathered in front of the hotel. They had learned that it had become Meade's headquarters. They came to serenade him and simply to say "thank you." Among the many links to the Civil War, it could be said that Frederick was the first to say "thank you" to George Gordon Meade and the Army of the Potomac.

Today we get worldwide news in moments. But that was not the case in 1863. The word was just reaching the people on July 7. Therefore, many cities held parades and celebrations the evening of July 7.

Meanwhile, trains were coming and going at Monocacy Junction. Rufus Ingalls, the quartermaster general of the North, was sending food, clothing and personal items for the troops. Along with everything else, 100 to 250 fresh horses came on the trains. Ingalls also had to send tons of grain and hay for the horses, as a supplement to what the horses consumed in the Maryland fields.

In New York City, there were riots. The draft had been instituted and was causing a lot of trouble. The riots had to be quelled. On July 8, Meade wrote a letter to his wife.

Headquarters Army of the Potomac, Frederick, July 8, 1863.

I arrived here yesterday; the army is assembling at Middletown. I think we shall have another battle before Lee can cross the river, though from all accounts he is making great efforts to do so. For my part, as I have to follow and fight him, I would rather do it at once and in Maryland than to follow in to Virginia. I received last evening your letters of the 3rd and 5th inst., and am truly rejoiced that you are treated with such distinction on account of my humble services. I see also that the papers are making a great deal too much fuss about me. I claim no extraordinary merit for this last battle, and would prefer waiting a little while to see what my career is to be before making any pretensions. I did and shall continue to do my duty to the best of my abilities, but knowing as I do that battles are often decided by accidents, and that no man of sense will say in advance what their result will be, I wish to be careful in not bragging before the right time. George [his son] is very well, though both of us are a good deal fatigued with our recent operations. From the time I took command till today, now over ten days, I have not changed my clothes, have not had a regular night's rest, and many nights not a wink of sleep, and for several days did not even wash my face and hands, no regular food, and all the time in a great state of mental anxiety. Indeed, I think I have lived as much in this time as in the last thirty years. Old Baldy is still living and apparently doing well; the ball passed within half an inch of my thigh, passed through the saddle and entered Baldy's stomach. I did not think he could live, but the old fellow has such a wonderful tenacity of life that I am in hopes he will.

The people in this place have made a great fuss with me. A few moments after my arrival I was visited by a deputation of ladies, and showers of wreaths and bouquets presented to me, in most complimentary terms. The street has been crowded with people, staring at me.[19]

Meade also received a letter from Washington. The sender was General Halleck, informing him that he had been appointed a brigadier general in the Regular Army, dating from July 3, the moment of "your brilliant victory at Gettysburg."

During the days of July 7 and 10, the infantry of the Army of the Potomac entered Frederick again. There was not the swagger of two weeks earlier, when they were headed north. The ranks were thinned. At the end of June, there had been 100,000 men in the ranks; now there were about 75,000. Nearly twice as many had fallen at Gettysburg as had been listed as killed, wounded or missing at Antietam. Some were ill from spending so much time in the rain, from having little to eat and from plain exhaustion. The First Corps, which had fought for a time west of Gettysburg, had been decimated. It would never be the same.

While there are many Union descriptions of events in Frederick en route to Gettysburg, accounts are lacking of the return. Perhaps that is due to the grief in the ranks, as they were missing so many comrades, or to the fatigue from "floundering in the mud" and getting soaked.

Major General Winfield Scott Hancock. *Library of Congress.*

On July 8, Jacob Engelbrecht watched the Twelfth Corps march through Frederick, headed for the mountains. He saw General Slocum, the corps commander, as well as about 750 Confederate prisoners. During the day, the various corps of the Army of the Potomac retraced their routes to the South Mountain passes: Crampton's, Fox's and Turner's. It was a miserable day, sometimes the sky turning as dark as night, with rolling thunder and flashes of light. The roads were steep and often very muddy. The horses had difficulties pulling the cannons.

Most of the units passed the body of the Confederate spy still dangling from a tree. The troops broke ranks and endeavored to boil coffee with whatever wet sticks they could find; some of the artillery had to be parked, and the horses had broken down.

By evening of July 9, Meade had departed Frederick and established his headquarters at the famous Mountain House at Turner's Gap.

The Potomac receded, and in mid-July, Lee was able to get his army across the river. However, in Gettysburg, Hagerstown and Frederick, as well as all along the routes taken by the troops, soldiers continued to die from wounds and illness.

Constant campaigning also took a toll on John Buford. Still a young man, he fell ill from days and nights in the saddle in the rain and cold or heat. Along with his infirmities, he grieved for the loss of a child and his father-in-law. He left the army on November 15 and died a month later. His funeral service was held on December 20. Among those in attendance was none other than President Abraham Lincoln. As the funeral procession proceeded from the church to the train, Buford's horse Gray Eagle followed the casket with an empty saddle and boots turned backward. Buford is buried at West Point.[20]

On June 28, 1930, the significance of the change of command in 1863 was marked along the road to Jefferson, at the base of Prospect Hall. A large boulder from Devil's Den commemorates Meade assuming command of the army.

June 1938 brought military units on the roads to Gettysburg passing through Frederick. These were horse-drawn wagons and cannons from Fort Meyer, carrying tents and supplies to Gettysburg for the seventy-fifth anniversary of the battle—the final reunion of the blue and gray. They were boys in the summer of 1863. Now they were in their nineties. Soon, many would answer "the last roll call."

Chapter 9

SPARED THE TORCH, 1864

The tide of the Confederacy crested at Antietam and then rose again the following summer at Gettysburg. However, with the retreat to Virginia, many in the South realized that it was just a matter of time until the superior manpower and supplies of the North would triumph.

Lincoln made a step to ensure this reality. In March 1864, he placed U.S. Grant in charge of all of the Union armies. Grant came east and moved with the Army of the Potomac. When the spring of 1864 arrived, the army crossed the Rapidan and moved toward the tangled underbrush of a wooded area called the Wilderness, west of Fredericksburg. During May 5–6, Grant suffered heavy losses. He could replace his men; Lee couldn't. The woods caught fire, and some of the wounded burned to death. When the fighting died down, the Confederates expected Grant to follow the path of the rest of the Union generals and retreat toward Washington. Late that night they heard sounds, but Grant was not retreating. Instead, he was heading south. Lee also placed his army in motion, and in mid-May battles raged around Spotsylvania Court House.

Again, Grant headed south, and for several weeks Lee with the interior lines kept one step ahead of Grant, until they reached the confines of Petersburg. There Grant kept extending his lines, and each extension depleted the ranks of the Army of Northern Virginia.

To ease the situation at Petersburg, Lee devised a daring plan. He would release the troops of Jubal Early from the Petersburg lines and send them to Lynchburg and into the Shenandoah Valley. Early could strike the forces of the notorious David Hunter, clear the valley and proceed north. Once in western Maryland, he could proceed to Frederick and then threaten Washington. Simultaneously, Bradley Johnson, a native Fredericktonian, would take a column of horsemen and endeavor to free the large number of Confederate prisoners held captive at Point Lookout, near the confluence of the Potomac River with the Chesapeake Bay. It was a daring plan, but if Early moved rapidly, it just might work. At this stage of the war, Lee had nothing to lose and everything to gain. Threatening Washington would relieve the pressure on Petersburg and could have major political consequences. The route to Monocacy, just like Antietam and Gettysburg, was via Frederick. One cannot dwell on the Battle of Monocacy without stressing the $200,000 ransom levied on Frederick, as well as the city being spared the torch.

There was a lot of anger with David Hunter. He had burned the Virginia Military Institute, books and all. Likewise, he had burned the home of John Letcher, Virginia's wartime governor. Hunter's action was in part responsible for the ransom on Frederick and, later, the burning of Chambersburg. The Confederacy felt that Hunter's actions were violations of warfare.

Commanding the Confederate forces approaching Frederick was Jubal Early, better known as "Old Jube." Born in 1816, Early graduated from West Point in 1837. He was against secession but had cast his lot with Virginia and was named the colonel of the Twenty-fourth Virginia. Promotions followed, and he served as a division commander under Richard Ewell. He succeeded that officer as commander of the Second Corps in the Army of Northern Virginia on May 29, 1864. Early was then given an independent command, which has become known as Early's Washington Raid.

Early's division commanders hailed from Kentucky, Georgia and North Carolina. None other than John Breckinridge commanded one of the divisions. After serving in the Kentucky legislature and the U.S. Congress, he became vice president under James Buchanan. At age thirty-five, he was one of several Democratic candidates for president, running against Abraham Lincoln in 1860. Breckinridge had to flee Kentucky when in October 1861 the federal government sought to capture him as a traitor. The year 1864 brought service with Jubal Early, and in the waning days of the Confederacy, Jefferson Davis named Breckinridge secretary of war.

John Brown Gordon was one of the outstanding figures of the war. Although having no military training, he excelled as a commander. Every inch an officer and a gentleman, he had the knack of inspiring his troops. Gordon graduated from the University of Georgia and became superintendent of a coal mine. The year 1861 found him as the commander of a company known as the Raccoon Roughs. Next he became colonel of the Sixth Alabama.

He was wounded several times at the Sunken Road at Antietam and led his troops in the other campaigns of the Army of Northern Virginia. His wife, Fannie, left their children with John's mother and traveled with her husband during the war. This was a source of great annoyance to "Old Jube." After the war, Gordon became governor of Georgia and then a U.S. senator. Fort Gordon, Georgia, is named after him.

Stephen Dodson Ramseur was born in North Carolina in 1836 and graduated from West Point, class of 1860. A brave leader, Ramseur was wounded at the Battles of Malvern Hill, Chancellorsville and Spotsylvania.

At Cedar Creek, he was mortally wounded and died the next day. Admiring Union officers and former West Point classmates paid their respects. Like Sandie Pendleton, he had been married less than a year and was given the news of the birth of a little girl just prior to being struck by Union bullets.

Robert Rodes had been a professor at VMI and had distinguished himself at Sharpsburg and Chancellorsville.

Early moved at an unbelievable pace, covering one hundred miles in four days and reaching Winchester on July 2. Frederick and the Monocacy River were fifty miles away.

John McCausland, Early's cavalry leader, rode to Martinsburg, tore up some tracks and disrupted communications. The damage was done to the Baltimore & Ohio tracks. John W. Garrett, the president of the railroad, so instrumental to the Federal war effort, was the first to notify the authorities in Washington that the Rebels had reached Martinsburg.

Dwelling on Hunter's actions in the Shenandoah, Early ordered his officers to make "requisitions or assessments" against certain towns. Receipts were to be given for supplies and cash collected. They would be happy to take "greenbacks."

The first to be faced with the Confederate demands was Hagerstown. John McCausland demanded $20,000 cash and 1,500 outfits of clothing.

Part of Early's army occupied Harpers Ferry, while Breckinridge and Confederate forces occupied Shepherdstown.

On July 5, prior to the crossing of the main body of troops, a column of horses splashed across Blackford's Ford. They were going to visit Ferry Hill Plantation. Douglas was taking Generals Early, Breckinridge, Gordon and Ramseur to meet his parents. On the afternoon of July 5, Breckinridge and Confederate troops crossed the Potomac into Maryland. Jubal Early made his headquarters on the old battlefield of Sharpsburg, while Bradley Johnson, the man entrusted with freeing Confederate prisoners, occupied Boonsboro.

Lew Wallace, hailing from Indiana, was in command of the Middle Military District, responsible for the defense of Delaware, Maryland and Washington. He was distressed when he received John Garrett's telegram. Wallace commanded a makeshift force known as the Eighth Army Corps, consisting of 2,500 men. Wallace asked the question: "What is to keep General Lee from marching to Washington?" The reply: "Nothing."

The next day, Wallace decided to go to Monocacy Junction, a key site just south of Frederick. He also learned that the Confederates had crossed the Potomac River and were in Washington County.

Realizing that streams were always an impediment to an enemy force and good for defense, Wallace checked the terrain and sent a message for some of his troops to take the train to Monocacy Junction. Wallace bedded down in the blockhouse. News arrived that some residents of Frederick, endeavoring to travel westward, were turned back by Confederate patrols.

Wallace said that although forts encircled Washington, he feared that President Lincoln would leave the White House by the back door while gray-clad officers entered the front door of the Executive Mansion.[1]

Wallace sent a telegram to U.S. Grant at City Point explaining the gravity of the situation. He stressed his plight and requested reinforcements. On the July 6, Grant ordered Major General James Rickets and five thousand troops of the Sixth Corps to Washington. The troops boarded ships, some sailing on the sixth, the rest the next day.

On the morning of July 8, the dusty, sweaty gray columns moved through the South Mountain passes into the fertile Middletown Valley. Early established his headquarters near the town. Early told town officials to pay him $5,000 at once or suffer the consequences of fire and destruction.

The burgess of Middletown urged Early to reduce the amount and give them more time. After all, they were a farming community.

"Old Jube" agreed to the reception of $1,500 by 7:00 a.m. the next day, plus another $3,500 from the rest of the election district. He received the $1,500 but did not wait for the rest of the money. His command was concentrating on Fredericktown. Later in the morning, Wallace saw with his field glasses the Confederates descending the Catoctin Mountains. However, he felt a little better. Some troops from the Sixth Corps had arrived in Washington and were sent immediately to assume defensive positions on the southeast bank of the Monocacy.

Henry Kyd Douglas, being familiar with Frederick, took command of the skirmishers as Early's army entered the western suburbs. He says that he was the first horseman in town. An enthusiastic citizen gave Douglas a handsome pair of spurs. Douglas was appointed the provost marshal of Frederick.[2]

Major General John Buford. *Library of Congress.*

The Honorable Edward S. Delaplaine shared the account of Dr. Robert T. Hammond describing the arrival of Jubal Early and the ransom of Frederick:

> *My father, Dr. Richard T. Hammond was at the time a practicing physician in Frederick. His residence was at the northwest corner of Market and Second Streets.*
>
> *A ring of the door bell was announced by my father, and three Confederate officers, the chief commander, General Jubal A. Early, being one of them, accosted my father with the urbanity characteristic of the Southern generals, and asked the privilege to do some writing within the residence, to which my father promptly consented.*
>
> *He [General Early] was ushered into the sitting room, and seated himself at a conventional drop-leaf walnut table.*
>
> *After finishing the writing he turned to my mother and said: "Madam, we are going to make a demand upon the banks of Frederick for $200,000, and if the demand is granted, very good, if not, Frederick will be reduced to ashes. We do this in retaliation for similar acts done by the Federal forces within our borders. You need not fear, as timely warning will be given you to leave with your family."*
>
> *My parents were both slave owners, and no doubt were pointed out from this fact as Southern sympathizers, which caused General Early to confide in them the demand they were going to make upon the banks of Frederick.*
>
> *My mother very frequently recalled the incident and pointed to the table whereon the historical demand was written and said that the table should be preserved.*[3]

The demand was undoubtedly prepared in the Hammond home. However, the note was not signed by Jubal Early. It bore the signature of four staff officers: Colonel William T. Allan, chief of ordnance; Major John A. Harman, chief quartermaster; Major J. Well Hawks, chief commissary; and Dr. Hunter McGuire, surgeon and medical director.

The demand said:

> *By order of the Lt. General, we require of the Mayor & town authorities of Frederick City Two Hundred thousand Dollars ($200,000.00)*

in current money for the use of this army. This contribution may be supplied by furnishing the Medical Dept. with Fifty thousand Dollars ($50,000.00) in stores at current prices: the Commissary Dept. with the stores to the same amount: the Ordnance Dept. with the same: and the Quarter Master's Dept. with a like amount.

Frederick was given the option of making its "contribution" either in cash or in "stores at current prices."

Major Hawks wrote another paper, specifying that he desired for the Commissary Department five hundred barrels of flour, six thousand pounds of sugar, three thousand pounds of coffee, three thousand pounds of salt and twenty thousand pounds of bacon.

The demand was taken to Mayor William G. Cole, who in turn sought the advice of Judge H. Marshall, a man who had studied in the office of Chief Justice Roger Brooke Taney and several others.

These folks appealed to the Confederates to be reasonable and merciful. After all, in 1864, $200,000 was a lot of money for a city with

Major General John Reynolds. *Library of Congress.*

a population of only eight thousand. They asked the Confederates to reconsider their demands. Of course, the answer was a firm "No." Arguing that Hagerstown had paid but $20,000, Early stated that McCausland had missed a zero and made a terrible mistake. Early also affirmed that unless the demands were met, Frederick would be burned. If necessary, he could be as brutal as General Hunter in the Shenandoah.

To expedite matters, Early sent young Sandie Pendleton, a former resident of Frederick, into the city to make sure that the levy would be paid. The city officials saw the dire circumstances. With the Union retreat, they had no choice—"pay or be burned." The mayor and the aldermen requested the banks to advance the money, giving them the assurance that "they would be reimbursed at the earliest possible moment." A resolution to this effect was then prepared:

> *Whereas, the Lieut. General Commanding the Confederate Army now occupying this Town has made a demand on the Corporate authorities for the sum of Two hundred thousand dollars ($200,000).*
>
> *And whereas, at a meeting of the Corporate authorities of said Town held this day, the following proceedings were had, with the concurrence and approval of the Citizens present.*
>
> *Resolved by the Mayor, Alderman & Common Council of Frederick, That the several Banking and Savings Institutions of the Town be requested to furnish so much of said sum of Two hundred thousand dollars pro rate according to their several & respective abilities and that the Corporate authorities will proceed at the earliest possible moment to reimburse said Banks and Savings Institutions, by levying upon the Citizens of said Corporation in proportion to their ability a sufficient tax to cover the same.*
>
> *Resolved, by the authority aforesaid, That the Mayor, Messrs. Sifford, Brunner, of the Board of Aldermen, Jno. A Simmons & T.M. Holbruner of the Board of Corn. Council & Joseph Baugher, R.H. Marshall, Lewis M. Nixdorff, Calvin Page and E. Albaugh, Esq. be authorized to demand said funds & pay over the same to the proper officer of said Army.*

Acting promptly upon the demand of Mayor Cole and his committee, the bank directors produced the cash. The following amounts were advanced by the five banks: by the Frederick Town Savings Institution, $64,000; by the Central Bank, $44,000; by the Frederick County Bank, $33,000; by the Franklin Savings Bank, $31,000; and by the Farmers and Mechanics Bank, $28,000.[4] The aggregate sum of $200,000 was then speedily turned over to the Confederate officers.

Major J.R. Braithwaite, quartermaster, gave the mayor a receipt "in full payment." The receipt reads as follows:

Frederick, July 9, 1864

Received of the Mayor, Alderman & Common Council of Frederick, the sum of Two hundred thousand dollars in full payment of said sum, which was this day levied and demanded to be paid to the Confederate States Army, by said Corporation of Frederick.

J.R. BRAITHWAITE
Maj. & Q.M.

One of the signers of the ransom note was Dr. Hunter Holmes McGuire. He was the son of a prominent Winchester physician and had attended Jefferson Medical School. Enlisting in the Second Virginia Infantry, he was appointed surgeon of the Stonewall Brigade and then surgeon of Jackson's entire command. McGuire had amputated Jackson's arm at Chancellorsville and then served under Ewell and Early. After the war, he became Richmond's leading physician. He was one of the first to advocate a National Department of Health and Welfare and, in the 1890s, was elected president of the American Medical Association. He also established the McGuire Clinic in Richmond. He was a prolific writer on medicine, the South and the Civil War. In 1904, a monument to his honor was placed on the Virginia state capitol grounds.[5]

William Allan, the chief of ordnance, was from Lexington, Virginia. After the war, he obtained notes from Jed Hotchkiss and wrote on the Shenandoah Valley campaign, as well as the Army of Northern Virginia. Allan also taught for many years at the McDonaugh School near Baltimore.

John A. Harman, the chief quartermaster, was from Staunton. A month younger than Jackson, he was a veteran of the Mexican-American

Lieutenant General Jubal Early (left) and Major General Lew Wallace. *Library of Congress.*

War. He was a big man, very loud and, at times, very profane. Beneath his gruff manner was a kindness, shown to his thirteen children. Two of them died while he served in the Army of Northern Virginia.

J. Wells Hawks was a businessman from Charles Town, Virginia, forty-three years old. Hawks had migrated from Massachusetts and had established a carriage business. Active in politics, Hawks had served as mayor of Charles Town, as well as in the state legislature. Hawks was the commissary officer.

While the Battle of Monocacy is not the focus of this book, it is briefly noted. The Monocacy River begins in southern Pennsylvania and meanders sixty miles through Frederick County before its confluence with the Potomac. The river is located east and south of Frederick and currently is one of primary source of the city's water supply.

Lew Wallace had placed troops on the east bank at the historic Jug Bridge on the National Road to Baltimore and then covered the roads to Washington.

Jed Hotchkiss, the premier cartographer of the Civil War, was among the Confederate ranks in July 1864. He had migrated from Windsor, New York, to Staunton. In March 1862, Jackson sent for him and said, "Mail me a map of the valley." This was the Shenandoah and was instrumental in Jackson's famed valley campaign.

Hotchkiss kept a wartime journal. For July 9, he writes:

> *Saturday—We went on to Frederick City…the enemy falling back to Monocacy Junction. We had some skirmishing and artillery practice before we reached the river. The enemy resisted our passage, most of the day, but McCaulsand dashed over their left and gained an important position, and Gordon followed with his division and flanked them, and drove them in gallant style: and about 1½ o'clock. Ramseur advanced on them…(Rodes also advanced) the route was complete. We crossed over and made our headquarters near the Junction…a levy of $200,000 was collected from Frederick City today.*[6]

In no man's land between the two armies were the Worthington and Thomas farms. Glenn Worthington was a lad of seven. He and the family took refuge in the basement, with the curious lad peering out of the basement windows to observe the unfolding action.

Later, the young boy became a prominent Frederick County judge and spearheaded efforts to have Monocacy become a national park. His book *Fighting for Time* is an eyewitness account of the Battle of Monocacy, which he says may have saved the Union.

While he fought for time, Wallace lost about 2,500 men. The Confederate loss was listed at 7,000. Many of the wounded of both sides were brought into Frederick for treatment—some were even placed in private homes.

Sandie Pendleton said that the city fathers haggled over the ransom, stalling for time and hoping for a Confederate defeat on the banks of the Monocacy, thus avoiding payment. To Sandie, with confidence in General Early and his comrades, that was wishful thinking. It was Pendleton who brought the news of the Confederate victory to the city fathers.

Sandie went to a prominent Frederick restaurant. There he dined with Allan, Hawks and Harman. They celebrated with a victory dinner. The exuberant Sandie noted: "I recall especially the ice cream seemed

Lieutenant General Early. *Library of Congress.*

delicious to us who had no such delicacies for a long time...the owner gave us champagne and we had a good time for an hour."[7]

Early regrouped on Sunday, July 10, and then marched southward to attack Washington. The heat and dust were terrible, and the men who had tramped from Lynchburg to Maryland suffered from thirst. Men dropped out of ranks by hundreds. They were within sight of the unfinished dome to the capitol and reached the Blair home, in what is now Silver Spring.

Early found the fortifications extremely strong. He also learned that Grant had sent veterans from the trenches of Petersburg to defend the city. It was during this time that President Lincoln came out to Fort Stevens to witness the action, only to be advised by a young officer, Oliver Wendell Holmes, to get down.

Early broke off the engagement and returned to Virginia. The third and last Confederate incursion into Maryland was over. Frederick was spared from the torch and Washington was saved.

Once again, the city of Frederick was flooded with the wounded of both sides, with the women of Fredericktown becoming once again "Angels of Mercy." Some, of course, did not make it; they, along with the Confederates killed in action in the fields along the Monocacy River, are buried at Mount Olivet Cemetery.

Early and his troops were disappointed. However, in a rare expression of humor, Early said to Douglas and the others: "We haven't taken Washington, but we've scared Abe Lincoln."

U.S. Grant wrote in his memoirs: "If Early had arrived one day earlier, he might have entered the capitol before the arrival of the reinforcements I had sent."[8]

Early had come so far and was so close to entering Washington. It's hard to imagine the results had he been successful. When he recrossed the Potomac into northern Virginia, there would be no more major Confederate incursions. Several weeks later, John McCausland entered into Pennsylvania. Chambersburg was not as fortunate as Frederick. The city was burned.

For the third time in three years, the Army of Northern Virginia had entered Maryland. The threat had to be stopped. As a result, U.S. Grant, the commander of all the Union armies, traveled to Monocacy Junction and then to the Thomas farm. There he met with Phil Sheridan. The generals mapped a strategy of total warfare. Sheridan was ordered to enter the Shenandoah Valley and destroy the Confederate army and lay waste to the Shenandoah Valley, burning the crops and barns, destroying the breadbasket of the Confederacy and breaking the people's will to fight.

There was a light moment at the Thomas farm. The daughter was asked whether her parents were Union or Southern sympathizers. She

The Confederate ransom note. *Frederick County Archives.*

replied, "When the Yankees are here, they are Yanks; when the Rebs are here, we are Rebs." This brought a laugh from General Grant.[9]

In September, Sheridan's columns departed Frederick for Harpers Ferry and Charles Town. At Berryville, Sheridan turned westward. The Battles of Third Winchester, Fisher's Hill and Cedar Creek followed. Early's army, the one that had marched from Lynchburg to Frederick and Washington, was decimated. The torch was applied to agricultural interests. It was Red October and the beginning of the end.

The Republican National Convention, meeting in Baltimore, renominated Lincoln. His opponent in the 1864 campaign was the former general George B. McClellan. The victories in the valley, and the vote of the soldiers, brought Lincoln's reelection.

On October 12, 1864, Roger Brooke Taney expired. He had held the office for a long time and had administered the oath of office to seven presidents: Martin Van Buren, William Henry Harrison, James K. Polk, Zachary Taylor, Franklin Pierce and, of course, Lincoln.

The City of Frederick's response to the ransom. *Frederick County Archives.*

Taney was buried at St. John's Cemetery in Frederick. His marker reads:

> *Roger Brooke Taney—Fifth Chief Justice of the United States of America, born in Calvert County, Maryland, March 17, 1777. Died in the city of Washington, October 12, 1864, aged 87 years, 6 mos., 25 days. He was a profound and able lawyer, and upright and fearless Judge, a pious and exemplary Christian at his own request, he was buried in a secluded spot near his mother. May he rest in peace.*

He is remembered for his *Dred Scott* decision—for one big event, rather than a lifetime of service. Monuments in his memory have been erected in Annapolis, Baltimore, Frederick, Ohio and in Taney County, Missouri. This famed jurist spent twenty-two years of his life in Frederick.

Meanwhile, Frederick city had principal and interest to pay on a $200,000 ransom. Finally, on September 29, 1951, eighty-seven years after Jubal Early demanded funds from the city of Frederick, the "last of the ransom fund was paid."

On October 1, 1951, the *Frederick Post* carried this story: "In ceremonies at City Hall and at Citizens National Bank, the liquidation of the old debt, incurred to keep General Jubal Early from sacking the city of July 9, 1864 was finally consummated."

City officials were uncertain as to the total cost of the ransom. Many felt that with the interest that had been paid over the years, the figure may have been pushed to $600,000.

Confederate receipt for the $200,000. *Frederick County Archives.*

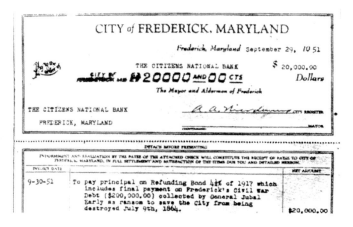

Paid in full. Frederick News Post, *October. 1, 1951.*

Mayor Donald Rice and the Frederick Board of Aldermen met at 10:00 a.m. on September 29 and signed a prepared statement in the presence of the media:

> *Four score and seven years ago, our forefathers covenanted to ransom Frederick city from Confederate devastation.*
>
> *Today we are met on behalf of this city to make final payment on that covenant made by our citizenry and their bankers.*
>
> *But in a larger sense we cannot repay, we cannot reimburse, that debt of gratitude and mutual trust:*
>
> *These brave men living and dead have imposed upon us by a continued and continuing mutual confidence, which existed then and shall endure forever, between administrations of this city, its citizens and its financial institutions.* [10]

The city officials, accompanied by the presidents of all of the local banks, then proceeded to the Citizens Bank to present the final payment. The check was carried in an old basket similar to the one in which the banks' cash quotas were carried to city hall in 1864. Each bank president symbolically carried a little basket.

At last the Confederate debt was paid in full.

Chapter 10

THE CENTENNIAL, 1961–1965

In the late 1950s, the State of Maryland formed a Civil War Centennial Commission. It was charged with planning appropriate events and ceremonies for the 100th anniversary of the Civil War. Frederick was to be involved. Three major events were scheduled for Frederick: a commemoration of the meeting of the Maryland legislature in 1861; the day of September 12, 1962, was designated as Frederick Day during the commemoration of the Maryland campaign of 1862; and events were planned connected with the Battle of Monocacy.

A proclamation was issued by the State of Maryland and, later, by the City of Frederick:

PROCLAMATION

WHEREAS, February 15, 1961 has been set apart to commemorate the 100th Anniversary of the "extra session" of the Maryland Legislature, held in Frederick, Maryland in 1861, and

WHEREAS, on this clay, a reenactment of this important meeting will be held by the citizens of Frederick City and County which will be of great historic importance and value to the people of this community, and

WHEREAS, Frederick City and County will be highly honored by the official visit of the Honorable J. Millard Tawes, Governor of Maryland

Glenn H. Worthington. *Frederick County Archives.*

and the members of the Maryland Legislature, in their first meeting outside Annapolis since the "extra session" 100 years ago, and

WHEREAS, *it is the earnest desire of the Mayor and Aldermen and the County Commissioners to extend a warm and cordial welcome to each of our distinguished guests and to provide every possible convenience for their comfort and enjoyment during their visit, and*

WHEREAS, *it is desired that all citizens of this community cooperate to the fullest extent to make this one of the most important events in the history of Frederick County.*

NOW THEREFORE, *we, Jacob R. Ramsburg, Mayor of Frederick City, and Delbert S. Null, President of the Commissioners of Frederick County, do hereby proclaim that February 15, 1961, be set apart and observed by the citizens of Frederick City and County in commemoration of the importance of the "extra session" of the Maryland Legislature to the ultimate outcome of the Civil War, and to the preservation of the Free State of Maryland in the Union.*

Done in the City and County of Frederick, State of Maryland, this 1st day of February, A.D. 1961.
Jacob R. Ramsburg, Mayor
Delbert S. Null, President

On February 15, 1961, all roads led to Frederick. Governor J. Millard Tawes and the members of the Maryland legislature descended on Frederick. The purpose was to remember the 1861 convening of the Maryland legislature in Frederick one hundred years prior.

Ceremonies began at 2:00 p.m. at the Francis Scott Key Hotel. The group then proceeded to the site of Kemp Hall, the scene of the 1861 legislative sessions. There Governor Tawes and the Honorable Edward S. Delaplaine dedicated a plaque remembering the days of long ago.

That night, a large crowd packed the Frederick Armory. Prior to World War II, the armory had been home to Company A and headquarters of the 115th Infantry, Maryland National Guard, a part of the famed 29th Blue Gray Division that landed on Omaha Beach on D-day, June 6, 1944.

The toastmaster was Frank Hennessey, a well-known TV personality from Baltimore. Letters were read from former president Dwight D. Eisenhower and President John F. Kennedy, expressing their regrets because they could not attend and wishing Marylanders well. Governor Tawes then made a few remarks, detailing the evolvement of the Maryland legislature. A Fredericktonian, and president of the Frederick County Historical Society, Congressman Charles McMathias then introduced the featured speaker, Major General Ulysses S. Grant III. Grant noted that Lincoln was keenly aware that the Maryland legislators might secede. However, he did not deem it proper to arrest them before they made a decision.

Reading a little-known letter from Lincoln, General Grant revealed that Lincoln had said: "It would not stop them to arrest or disperse them. We must only await their action and we must use the suspension of the writ of habeas corpus only in an extreme emergency."

In individual and national life, there are always the "what ifs." The fate of the nation may have hung in the balance in Frederick in 1861. Some will recall the days of the Berlin airlift, when supplies had to be flown daily into the city as the Russians refused ground movement. Had Maryland withdrawn from the Union, Washington would nearly have

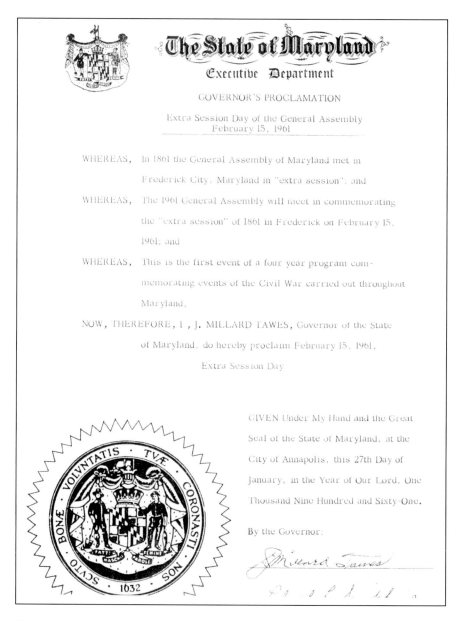

The centennial proclamation. *Centennial program booklet.*

been an island, too, surrounded by the Confederacy on the north, west and south. The only avenue of supply and commerce would have been the Potomac River and the Chesapeake. So the question of "What if Maryland had seceded" loomed on the horizon.

Following is the program planned for February 15, 1961:

7:00 P.M.—BANQUET—Armory—(Admission by Ticket Only)
Toastmaster—Frank Hennessy, Baltimore, Maryland
Presentation of Colors—Girl Scout Troop No. 7—Directed by Mrs. Irvin F. Stride
Star Spangled Banner—Civil War Songs—Hood College Choral Group
Welcome to Frederick City—Mayor Jacob R. Ramsburg
Welcome to Frederick County—President Delbert S. Null, County Commissioners
Introduction of Governor—Senator Samuel W. Barrick
Remarks—Governor J. Millard Tawes
Introduction of Speaker—Congressman Charles McMathias, Jr., President, Frederick County Historical Society
Guest Speaker—Major-General Ulysses S. Grant, III

On the morning of February 16, these were the lead stories in the *Frederick News Post*:

LEGISLATORS HONORED AT DINNER HERE
Grandson of General Grant Addresses Event At Armory
Messages received from Ike, Kennedy

CENTENNIAL OBSERVANCE OF CIVIL WAR
Lawmakers Quickly Authorize $2,500 Appropriation
Kemp Hall Plaque Unveiled by Tawes

The next big event was the remembrance of Robert E. Lee's Maryland campaign of 1862. The first major event was the rededication of the rebuilt Dunker Church on the Antietam Battlefield. Nightly, a historical pageant, *The Hills of Glory*, was presented in Hagerstown, and there was a reenactment of the Battle of Antietam near the new Visitor's Center, which was still under construction. Every town in the area had a special

The Confederate grave, Mount Olivet. *Author's collection.*

The Centennial, 1961–1965

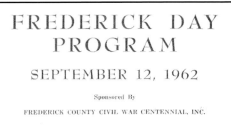

Right: Frederick Day, 1962. *Centennial program booklet.*

Below: Booklet for the 100th anniversary commemoration of the Battle of Monocacy. *Centennial program booklet.*

FREDERICK DAY
PROGRAM

SEPTEMBER 12, 1962

Sponsored By

FREDERICK COUNTY CIVIL WAR CENTENNIAL, INC.

In Cooperation With

THE ANTIETAM-SOUTH MOUNTAIN CENTENNIAL, INC.

Commemorating

THE HISTORICAL EVENTS OF
THE CIVIL WAR
IN FREDERICK AND WASHINGTON COUNTIES

NATIONAL
CENTENNIAL CEREMONY

At the Pennsylvania Monument

SUNDAY, JULY 5, 1964
3 P. M.

"THE STAR-SPANGLED BANNER"
Aberdeen Proving Ground Army Band
INVOCATION   Rev. David Dawson
Pastor, Araby Methodist Church
"The Battlefield Church"
MASTER OF CEREMONIES   General James Davenport
United States Army, Ret
WELCOME FROM THE CITY
OF FREDERICK   Hon. E. Paul Magaha
Mayor of Frederick
WELCOME FROM THE COUNTY
OF FREDERICK   Hon. A. Irvin Renn
President, Frederick County Commissioners
GREETINGS FROM THE MARYLAND CIVIL
WAR CENTENNIAL COMMISSION   E. Leister Mobley, Jr.
Chairman, Executive Committee
MESSAGE FROM HON. J. MILLARD TAWES,
GOVERNOR OF MARYLAND   C. Lease Bussard
President, Frederick County Civil War Centennial, Inc.
MESSAGE FROM HON. RICHARD J. HUGHES,
GOVERNOR OF NEW JERSEY   Hon. William M. Beard
Member, New Jersey Civil War Centennial Commission
MESSAGE FROM HON. WILLIAM W. SCRANTON,
GOVERNOR OF PENNSYLVANIA   Dr. Sylvester K. Stevens
Executive Director, Pennsylvania Historical and Museum Commission
MESSAGE FROM HON. PHILIP H. HOFF,
GOVERNOR OF VERMONT   Thomas A. Chadwick
Chester, Vermont
MESSAGE FROM NEW YORK STATE DIVISION OF MILITARY
AND NAVAL AFFAIRS Lieut. Colonel Donald G. Brossman
INTRODUCTION OF THE STAFF OF THE
SONS OF VETERANS   Lieut. Col. Chester Shriver
Past National Commander, Sons of Veterans
SELECTION   Aberdeen Proving Ground Army Band
ADDRESS   Hon. Theodore R. McKeldin
Mayor of Baltimore, Former Governor of Maryland
PLACING OF WREATH   Mayor McKeldin
Escorted by General W. A. Morgan, Judge Edward S. Delaplaine,
Colonel Raymond B. Ward, Dr. Irwin Richman, Assistant Historian,
Commonwealth of Pennsylvania
FIRING SQUAD AND TAPS
"AMERICA, THE BEAUTIFUL"
Aberdeen Proving Ground Army Band
BENEDICTION   Lieut. Col. Herbert Rounds

SOUVENIR PROGRAMME

COMMEMORATION OF THE
100th ANNIVERSARY
OF THE

BATTLE OF MONOCACY

Maryland Marker, Monocacy Battlefield

AND THE

DEDICATION
OF THE

MARYLAND CIVIL WAR MARKER

Sponsored by
FREDERICK COUNTY CIVIL WAR CENTENNIAL, INC.
In Co-operation With
THE MARYLAND CIVIL WAR CENTENNIAL COMMISSION

JULY 5 and 9, 1964

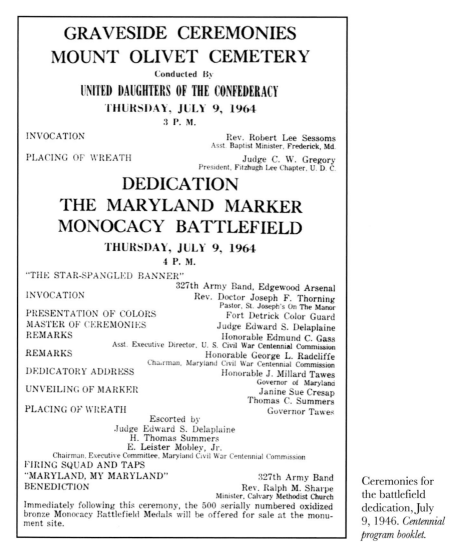

GRAVESIDE CEREMONIES
MOUNT OLIVET CEMETERY
Conducted By
UNITED DAUGHTERS OF THE CONFEDERACY
THURSDAY, JULY 9, 1964
3 P. M.

INVOCATION   Rev. Robert Lee Sessoms
                              Asst. Baptist Minister, Frederick, Md.

PLACING OF WREATH   Judge C. W. Gregory
                          President, Fitzhugh Lee Chapter, U. D. C.

DEDICATION
THE MARYLAND MARKER
MONOCACY BATTLEFIELD
THURSDAY, JULY 9, 1964
4 P. M.

"THE STAR-SPANGLED BANNER"
                              327th Army Band, Edgewood Arsenal
INVOCATION   Rev. Doctor Joseph F. Thorning
                              Pastor, St. Joseph's On The Manor
PRESENTATION OF COLORS   Fort Detrick Color Guard
MASTER OF CEREMONIES   Judge Edward S. Delaplaine
REMARKS   Honorable Edmund C. Gass
            Asst. Executive Director, U. S. Civil War Centennial Commission
REMARKS   Honorable George L. Radcliffe
            Chairman, Maryland Civil War Centennial Commission
DEDICATORY ADDRESS   Honorable J. Millard Tawes
                                    Governor of Maryland
UNVEILING OF MARKER   Janine Sue Cresap
                                    Thomas C. Summers
PLACING OF WREATH   Governor Tawes
                      Escorted by
              Judge Edward S. Delaplaine
                  H. Thomas Summers
                  E. Leister Mobley, Jr.
        Chairman, Executive Committee, Maryland Civil War Centennial Commission
FIRING SQUAD AND TAPS
"MARYLAND, MY MARYLAND"   327th Army Band
BENEDICTION   Rev. Ralph M. Sharpe
                          Minister, Calvary Methodist Church
Immediately following this ceremony, the 500 serially numbered oxidized
bronze Monocacy Battlefield Medals will be offered for sale at the monu-
ment site.

Ceremonies for the battlefield dedication, July 9, 1946. *Centennial program booklet.*

day. The day for Frederick was September 12, the day the Union troops entered the city in 1862. Windows were decorated with 1862 themes. There was a big parade, and the visit of General Reno to Barbara Fritchie was portrayed.

Additional ceremonies were held in July 1964, commemorating the Battle of Monocacy, Frederick Day.

In 1974, Congressman Goodloe Byron introduced a bill to expand the 1934 legislation for the Monocacy National Battlefield. At last, on July

13, 1991, the park just south of Frederick was dedicated, and on June 27, 2007, a new modern Visitor's Center was dedicated.

For Frederick's Civil War Centennial, the reader is referred to Frederick County Archives and to the Frederick News Post, *February 16, 1961, and September 1962 issues and the July 10, 1964 issue.*

Chapter 11

FREDERICK REMEMBERS

Frederick, more than 250 years old, older than our nation, grew from a hamlet at the crossroads of two Indian trails; it has grown to have a population of more than fifty thousand people and is one of Maryland's most important cities. Although modern and upbeat, the city retains the quaint charm of days gone by.

But the city fathers and Frederick County Tourism have remembered the past. The visitor is urged to begin his or her visit at the tourism office located on East Church Street or at the new facility located near the train station off East Patrick Street.

Entering Frederick from I-70 and proceeding into Frederick on South Market Street, the visitor will pass Mount Olivet Cemetery. Standing at the entrance to the cemetery, on your left is the statue and memorial to Francis Scott Key, the distinguished lawyer and composer of our national anthem.

Atop the monument is a bronze statue of Key, while at the base there are three figures representing patriotism, war and music. Other notables buried at Mount Olivet are Barbara Fritchie and Thomas Johnson, the first governor of Maryland.

Located along a fence at the western edge of the cemetery are stones representing the burial of 408 Confederates who either fell at Monocacy or died of wounds after Antietam or while they were imprisoned in Frederick. The burial list is at the Antietam National Battlefield.

The opening of the Monocacy National Battlefield. *Left to right*: Superintendant Susan Moore, Governor William Donald Schaefer and Congresswoman Beverly Byron. *Author's collection.*

Few are aware of it, but near the graves of the men who wore the gray—and who fell far from home and loved ones by a river with a strange-sounding name—is a sixteen-foot granite shaft. The Confederate Memorial was erected by the Ladies Monument Commission of Frederick County in honor of the soldiers of the Confederate army who fell in the Battle of Monocacy and elsewhere. Normally, services are held on Confederate Memorial Day, June 6.

The monument, erected in 1880, has this inscription: "Soldier rest, the warfare o'er…Dream of battled fields no more, day of anger, nights of waking."

At the end of the long line of graves is a big stone set in memory of all the unknowns: someone's husband, brother, neighbor or sweetheart, known "but to God."

We, too, can remember as we step back in time and recall those who have gone before. Perhaps we might sense the vibrations of Daniel and Patrick Dulaney, George Washington, Benjamin Franklin, Edward Braddock, the Hessians, Lewis and Clark, the Frederick militia, Roger

Brooke Taney, the 1861 legislature, Ambrose Burnside, Wilder Dwight, Robert E. Lee, Stonewall Jackson, Barbara Fritchie, Jesse Lee Reno, Rutherford B. Hayes, William McKinley, Edward and Paul Revere, the troops of the Iron Brigade and Stonewall Brigade, George G. Meade, John and Catherine Reynolds, George A. Custer, Jubal Early, Lew Wallace, Glenn Worthington and a host of others.

During the Civil War, Frederick was "one vast hospital." One, of course, was at the Hessian barracks on the current grounds of Maryland School for the Deaf. This was a general hospital. Likewise for the U.S. Hotel on the southwest corners of South Market and All Saints Streets, 101–107 South Market. It was erected in the early 1800s and served as Meade's headquarters after Gettysburg. Now there are apartments. The City Hotel, built in 1803, was demolished to make room for the Francis Scott Key Hotel in 1921. Most of the churches were employed, including the German Reformed, the Lutheran church with its twin spires and the Presbyterian church. A picture remains of the Lutheran hospital. A complete listing can be obtained from the National Museum of Civil War Medicine.

Leaving Mount Olivet Cemetery, the visitor should proceed north on South Market Street. Just after the first traffic light, Maryland School for the Deaf stands on the right or eastern corner. On the grounds of the school are the famed Hessian barracks, erected in 1777. Periodically, there are living history programs presented here. There is also a museum.

On the southeast corner is the B&O railroad station. Lincoln departed from the station and made a speech to the residents of Frederick on October 4, 1862.

At the intersection of Market and Patrick Streets, the principal avenues in Frederick, Union and Confederate cavalry clashed on September 1862; both armies turned onto West Patrick Street, eventually reaching Antietam. General McClellan was mobbed by admiring Fredericktonians at this intersection. And on the northeast corner is the store where Confederate soldiers stood in line to obtain hats.

On the southeast corner of North Market and East Church Streets is Kemp Hall, owned by the former German Reformed Church and site of the meeting of the Maryland legislature in 1861.

A few yards down on East Church Street is the Frederick County Tourism office and Visitor's Center. This is worth a stop.

Walking left on West Church Street, you can see the spire of Trinity Church and the famed clock. This was from the original German Reformed Church. Across the street, the brick structure is the house of worship erected in 1842, the place where Stonewall Jackson attended services on the evening of Sunday, September 7, 1862.

A few yards west is Courthouse Square, with the bust of Roger Brooke Taney. Nearby is the site of a building that served as law offices for Roger Brooke Taney and Francis Scott Key.

To the rear of the old courthouse, now city hall, is Record Street and the Ramsay House, the place where General Hartsuff was treated and where he was visited by President Lincoln.

A block north of Courthouse Square is the Presbyterian church, which was a hospital. Some of the walking wounded made their way to the Ramsay House to see Mr. Lincoln.

Going south on Court Street, one passes All Saints Episcopal Church, served by William Nelson Pendleton, 1846–54.

On West Patrick Street is the home of Barbara Fritchie, subject of the immortal poem. And a half-mile south on Bentz Street is the home and museum of Roger Brooke Taney. Among the featured items is the table on which Taney wrote the *Dred Scott* decision.

Three plantation-style properties are also a part of Frederick's Civil War heritage. Only one, Rose Hill Manor, is open to the public.

Near Butterfly Lane is Prospect Hall, headquarters for the Army of the Potomac, June 27–29, 1863, and the place where George G. Meade assumed command of the Army of the Potomac. It is private property.

On North Market Street, just beyond Thomas Johnson High School, is Rose Hill Manor. This was the home of Thomas Johnson, the first governor of Maryland. Union soldiers camped here during the winter of 1861–62. It was the locale of many army reviews. John Reynolds may have had his headquarters here the night of June 28, 1863. Rose Hill Manor has a fine children's museum. It hosts a Civil War encampment in the summer and also a fall festival.

Three miles north of Frederick is Richfield. It was a farm visited by George Washington and the home of Admiral Winfield Scott Schley, a naval hero of the Spanish-American War. In 1863, it was a Union cavalry camp. It was here that George A. Custer assumed command of a brigade of Michigan cavalry.

So take your time. Stop and smell the roses. Tour Frederick, the Monocacy Battlefield, the National Museum of Civil War Medicine and the other sites connected with Frederick, the crossroads of the Civil War.

Adding to the lore of the past and enriching the present is one of Frederick's newest museums, a facility that has gained national attention. Through the years, Dr. Gordon Dammann of Illinois had amassed perhaps the most formable collection of Civil War medicine artifacts in the United States. Being somewhat far removed in the Midwest, he dreamed of a facility in the East, in the heart of Civil War country. He, along with this writer and others, checked several sites at Antietam. However, there were problems with location and security.

Then, on a rainy summer day, Gordon and several friends traveled to Frederick. Mayor Paul Gordon and others greeted him warmly. They toured the city and found a vacant structure on East Patrick Street. Lo and behold, the place had been a Civil War hospital and temporary morgue. It had been one of the sites selected by Dr. Jonathan Letterman, one of Gordy's heroes and the medical director of the army, as a place to receive the wounded from Antietam.

The rest is history. With the assistance of many, the museum became a reality. The building now houses the Dammann Collection and is a state-of-the-art museum. The National Museum of Civil War Medicine has working arrangements with nearby Fort Detrick, Hood College, the federal government and a host of others. The museum has also opened a branch at the Pry farm, just east of Antietam National Battlefield. The Pry farm was the location of McClellan's headquarters, September 15–20, and was a field hospital. The museum is located at 48 East Patrick Street.

The curtain of life has fallen on the Fredericktonians of 1862, as well as the columns of blue and gray who camped and marched in the shadows of the "clustered spires."

The bugles are quiet. No more do we hear the beat of the drums, the shouts of command, the *tramp-tramp* of marching feet or the rumble of cannons. The weapons are stacked and the flags are furled. But perhaps "in the evening dews and damps," we might reflect on the days of the 1860s and those moments when Frederick was at the crossroads of the Civil War.

NOTES

CHAPTER 1

1. Edward S. Delaplaine, the late judge, was one of Frederick's most prominent citizens. In addition to a distinguished legal career, he was one of Maryland's premier historians, writing on Francis Scott Key, Governor Thomas Johnson, Roger B. Taney and Frederick County. He was an advocate of the creation of the Monocacy Battlefield. However, he was never too busy to help aspiring young writers—including this one.

2. Wentz, *The Lutheran Church in Frederick County, Maryland*. For additional information on Frederick, the reader is referred to the many writings of Paul Gordon and his wife, Rita. The former mayor has written extensively on his beloved city, including the textbook *History of Frederick County*. This book is used in county schools.

CHAPTER 2

1. For more on the political intrigue leading to the Civil War, see Bruce Catton, *The Coming Fury*.

2. Greene, *The Raid*, 82.

3. Oswald Garrison Villard, *John Brown a Biography, Fifty Years After* (1909).

4. Ibid.

5. Greene, *The Raid*, 82–91.

6. Quoted in many newspapers.

CHAPTER 3

1. *Frederick Examiner*, September 18, 1861.

2. Quaife, *Letters from the Cannon's Mouth*, letter, December 1861.

3. Ibid. Williams letter dated December 7, 1861.

4. Ibid.

5. Quint, *Life and Letters of Wilder Dwight*, December 1861 and January 1862.

6. Brown, *Twenty Seventh Indiana Volunteer Infantry*, 77–79.

7. Quint, *Life and Letters of Wilder Dwight*, December 21, 1861.

8. Ibid. Letter dated December 23, 1861.

9. Quint, *Life and Letters of Wilder Dwight*, January 18, 1862.

CHAPTER 4

1. *War of the Rebellion* (hereafter *OR*). The fundamental published primary source on the Antietam campaign. The reports and correspondence of Maryland operations are found in ser. I, vol. 19, pts. 1 and 2.

2. Ibid.

3. Scharff, *History of Western Maryland*, vol. 1, 282.

4. Jacob Engelbrecht Diaries, September 6, 1862.

5. Evans, *Confederate Military History*, vol. 2, 90.

6. Murfin, *Gleam of Bayonets*. Murfin, while doing research on his book, discovered the unpublished photograph of Confederate soldiers lining up for hats.

7. Douglas, *I Rode with Stonewall*, 149.

8. Ibid.

9. *OR*, vol. 19, pt. 2, 601–5.

10. Ibid.

11. Blackford, *War Years with Jeb Stuart*, 1946.

12. Ibid.

13. Douglas, *I Rode with Stonewall*, 151.

14. McDonald, *Make Me a Map of the Valley*, notes for September 10, 1862.

15. Southern Historical Society Papers (SHSP), vol. 10, 500.

16. Ibid., 508–9.

17. Jacob Engelbrecht Diaries, September 10, 1862.

18. Ibid.

19. Dooley, *John Dooley, Confederate Soldier: His War Journal*, 36.

20. Catherine Susannah Thomas Markell recorded a journal from 1856 to 1898. Her diary for September 1862 is a jewel. September 5 brought the exciting news that the Army of Northern Virginia was approaching Fredericktown. On September 6, Marylanders Bradley Johnson and Henry Kyd Douglas entered Frederick on South Market Street. These were the first Confederates whom Mrs. Markell witnessed. She records the fact that Johnson worshiped at the German Reformed Church on September 7. And on Monday, General William Barksdale and staff dined at the Markell home. Catherine sent a basket of fruit to Jubal Early. These were "fine pears tied up in a red bandana." The Markells accepted small groups of Southern soldiers into their store to make purchases. Later in the day, Generals Lafayette McLaws and Joseph Kershaw dined with the Markells, while orderlies stood outside holding the reins of the horses. September 9 was a gala day for Mrs. Markell, visiting the camps south of Frederick; she had the privilege of meeting Generals Lee, Jackson and Longstreet. She noticed that Lee's wrists were bandaged almost to the tips of his fingers. He said, "Touch them gently, ladies, touch them gently." On September 12, Mrs. Markell hosted General Stuart and Wade Hampton. The tide turned on September 13, and Federal cavalry searched the Markell home. On September 14, men in blue marched by the Markell home, and the premises were searched once again.

21. Douglas, *I Rode with Stonewall*, 134.

22. Jacob Engelbrecht Diaries, September 13, 1862.

23. Johnson, *Long Roll*, 182.

24. Graham, *Ninth Regiment*, 260–61. Also known as *Hawkins Zouaves*.

25. McClellan, *McClellan's Own Story*, 571.

26. Ibid., 572.

27. Strother, *Virginia Yankee in the Civil War*. This is a compilation of Strother's wartime journal. See notes for September 13, 1862.

28. Silas Colgrove, "The Finding of Lee's Lost Order," *Battles and Leaders*, vol. 2, 563.

29. Gibbon, *Personal Recollections of the War*, 73.

30. Dawes, *Service with the Sixth Wisconsin Volunteers*, 79. A classic story of a regiment in the famed Iron Brigade.

31. Gibbon, *Personal Recollections of the War*, 74.

32. Jonathan Stowe's journal was found at the Hoffman Farm hospital, where he died from wounds received at Antietam. Vertical file, Antietam National Battlefield Library.

33. Page, *History of the Fourteenth Regiment*, 27.

34. Sawyer, *Military History of the Eighth*, 77.

35. Livermore, *Days and Events*, 119.

36. From accounts of the 125th Pennsylvania Volunteers, vertical file, Antietam National Battlefield. The general expired under a tree known as the Reno Oak. It stood until the 1970s, when it was blown over in a storm.

Chapter 5

1. *Middletown Valley Register*, October 10, 1862.

2. Delaplaine, *Lincoln and His Traveling Companions*. The honorable judge was the first to write on Lincoln's visit to Antietam. See also Schildt, *Four Days in October*.

3. The speeches were quoted in Scharff, *History of Western Maryland*, vol. II, 259.

4. Ibid.

CHAPTER 6

1. Barbara Fritchie shared the account in this book with Miss Caroline Ebert, her husband's niece, in the period between September 1862 and Barbara's death in December. Miss Ebert shared the account with Mrs. J.H. Abbott and Eleanor Abbott, testifying to the truth of the story.

2. Continuation of Barbara Fritchie's account shared with relatives.

CHAPTER 7

1. Bean, *Stonewall's Man*, 43.

2. Lee, *Memoirs of William Nelson Pendleton*; Pendleton Papers, the University of North Carolina.

3. Pendleton Papers, letters from Nelson to wife, June 18 and June 25, 1863.

4. The river crossing south of Shepherdstown was a gateway to the Shenandoah Valley. It was known as Pack Horse, Blackford's and also Boteler's Ford. It was one crossing with three names.

CHAPTER 8

1. For years, mystery surrounded the Confederate spy Harrison, and then his true identity was revealed. In 1986, James O. Hall wrote an article for *Civil War Times Illustrated*. In the National Archives, he found the

identity of the James Longstreet's famous but mysterious spy. Henry Thomas Harrison had joined the Confederacy in Mississippi. His skills soon became apparent, and Harrison was selected for top-secret work. Harrison was born near Nashville in 1832. His original enlistment was with the Twelfth Mississippi Infantry. He was assigned to spy for James Longstreet on March 7, 1863. Shortly thereafter, he was arrested and narrowly escaped execution. In June 1863, he trailed the Army of the Potomac to Frederick and then made haste to report to Lee the news of the Union change of command and the location of the Army of the Potomac. In September 1863, Harrison married Laura Borders. The marriage did not last, and little is known about the succeeding years. Harrison died on October 28, 1923, and is buried at the Highland Cemetery in Fort Mitchell, Kentucky.

2. Meade, *Life and Letters of George Gordon Meade*, vol. 2, 13.

3. Charles C. Coffin, *Boston Globe*, July 1863.

4. Charles F. Benjamin, "Hooker's Appointment and Removal," *Battles and Leaders*, vol. 3, 500. The change of command is also noted in Powell, *Fifth Army Corps*.

5. The promotion of the three young captains, including George A. Custer, is found in *OR*, 926, and also in Pleasonton, *Annals of the War*, 452.

6. Gerrish, *Army Life*, 95–96.

7. *OR*, pt. 2, 426.

8. *OR*, pt. 3, 370.

9. Houghton, *Campaigns of the Seventeenth Maine*, 82.

10. Trobriand, *Four Years with the Army*, 525.

11. Marbaker, *Eleventh New Jersey Volunteers*, 89.

12. Slocum, *Life and Services of Major General Henry Warner Slocum.*

13. Catherine Reynolds, the cousin of Major General John Fulton Reynolds, lived in an L-shaped house at 9 West Second Street. The structure was to be demolished in 1925.

14. Abner Doubleday went by Rose Hill Manor. The artillery reserve of the Army of the Potomac was encamped at Rose Hill Manor, the former home of Governor Thomas Johnson. On the grounds of this historic plantation were 110 cannons—along with the more than two thousand animals needed to pull them along the road—and 745 artillerymen.

15. Lieutenant James Stewart of Battery B, Fourth U.S. Artillery, rode "Old Tartar," the horse without a tail; Stewart was shot off the horse at Second Manassas.

16. Meade, contained in *OR*, pt. 3, 458–59.

17. Meade, *Life and Letters of George Gordon Meade*, vol. 2, letter dated July 7–8, 1863.

18. *New York Times*, July 13, 1863.

19. Meade, *Life and Letters of George Gordon Meade*, vol. 2, 13.

20. For more information on Buford, see Longacre, *General John Buford.*

Chapter 9

1. For more on the Battle of Monocacy, see Cooling, *Jubal Early's Raid*. A distinguished military historian, Cooling has been a lifelong student of this battle. Another must-read is the eyewitness account of Glenn H. Worthington, *Fighting for Time.*

2. Douglas, *I Rode with Stonewall*, 293.

3. From the research of Judge Edward S. Delaplaine and from the Frederick County Archives.

4. Frederick County Archives. At the time of the ransom, city hall was located at 124 North Market Street. It became an opera house and is now a restaurant.

5. See Schildt, *Doctor in Gray*. This is a biography of Stonewall Jackson's physician.

6. Hotchkiss Journal, July 7–9, 1864.

7. Bean, *Stonewall's Man*, 206.

8. Grant, *Memoirs of U.S. Grant*, vol. 2, 305.

9. *Frederick News Post*, October 1, 1951.

10. From a Frederick city document, appearing in the *Frederick News Post*, October 1, 1951, as well as in other print media across the country.

BIBLIOGRAPHY

PRIMARY SOURCES

Adams County Archives, Pennsylvania, Gettysburg.

Engelbrecht Diaries, Frederick County Archives, Frederick, Maryland.

Frederick County Archives, Frederick, Maryland.

Frederick Examiner, Frederick, Maryland, 1849–1890, Frederick County Archives.

Frederick News Post, Frederick Maryland, 1951–2010, Frederick News Post Archives.

Henry Kyd Douglas Papers, Bast Museum, Boonsboro, Maryland.

Jed Hotchkiss Journal, Library of Congress, Washington, D.C.

Lutheran Church Archives, Gettysburg, Maryland.

New York Times, July 13, 1863.

William Nelson Pendleton Papers, Southern Historical Society, University of North Carolina.

Secondary Sources

Bean, W.G. *Stonewall's Man: Sandie Pendleton.* Chapel Hill, NC: University of North Carolina Press, 1959.

Blackford, William Willis. *The War Years with Jeb Stuart.* Whitefish, MT: Kessinger Publishing, 1946.

Brown, Edmund. *The Twenty Seventh Indiana Volunteer Infantry in the War of the Rebellion.* N.p.: General Books LLC, 1899.

Catton, Bruce. *The Coming Fury.* New York: Phoenix Press, 2001.

Child, William. *A History of the Fifth Regiment New Hampshire Volunteers.* Charleston, SC: Nabu Press, 1893.

Cooling, Frank. *Jubal Early's Raid on Washington.* N.p.: Fire Ant Books, 2008.

Cunz, Deiter. *The Maryland Germans.* Princeton, New Jersey, 1948.

Dawes, Rufus. *Service with the Sixth Wisconsin Volunteers.* Marietta, OH: Alderman and Sons, n.d.

Delaplaine, Edward S. *Lincoln and His Traveling Companions to Antietam.* Harrogate, Tennessee, n.d.

Dooley, John. *John Dooley, Confederate Soldier: His War Journal.* Edited by Joseph Durkin. Washington, D.C.: Georgetown University Press, 1945.

Douglas, Henry Kyd. *I Rode with Stonewall.* Chapel Hill, NC: University of North Carolina Press, 1940.

Evans, Clement A., ed. *Confederate Military History.* Richmond, VA: Confederate Publishing Company, 1899.

Freeman, Douglas S. *Lee's Lieutenants.* 3 vols. New York: Scribner, 1942–44.

Gerrish, Theodore. *Army Life: A Private's Reminiscences of the Civil War.* Charleston, SC: Nabu Press, 2010.

Gibbon, John. *Personal Recollections of the War.* New York: Putnam's, 1928.

Gordon, Paul, and Rita Gordon. *History of Frederick County.* Frederick, MD: Board of Education of Frederick County, 1975.

Graham, Matthew J. *The Ninth Regiment New York Volunteers.* New York: Coby & Company, 1905.

Grant, U.S. *Memoirs of U.S. Grant.* New York: Charles Webster, 1885.

Greene, Laurence. *The Raid: A Biography of Harpers Ferry.* New York: Holt, 1960.

Holt, John R. *Historic Frederick.* N.p.: Marken & Bielfeld, 1949.

Houghton, Edwin D. *The Campaigns of the Seventeenth Maine.* College Station, TX: Southern Methodist University Press, 1886.

Johnson, Charles. *The Long Roll.* Ann Arbor: University of Michigan Library, 1911.

Johnson, Robert E., and Clarence Buel. *Battles and Leaders of the Civil War.* 4 vols. New York: Century Company, 1884–87.

Lee, Susan P., ed. *The Memoirs of William Nelson Pendleton.* Charleston, SC: Nabu Press, 2010.

Livermore, Thomas L. *Days and Events, 1860–65.* Boston: Houghton and Mifflin, 1920.

Longacre, Edward. *General John Buford: A Military Biography.* Conshohocken, PA: Combined Books, 1995.

Marbaker, Thomas. *The Eleventh New Jersey Volunteers*. College Station, TX: Southern Methodist University Press, 1892.

McClellan, George B. *McClellan's Own Story*. New York: Webster, 1887.

McDonald, Archie, ed. *Make Me a Map of the Valley: Jackson's Cartographer*. College Station, TX: Southern Methodist University Press, 1973.

Meade, George G. *The Life and Letters of George Gordon Meade*. Vol. 2. Edited by George Meade, grandson. New York: Scribner, 1923.

Murfin, James. *The Gleam of Bayonets*. New York: Thomas Yoseloff, 1965.

Page, Charles. *History of the Fourteenth Regiment Connecticut Volunteers*. Boston, MA: Horton Printing Company, 1884.

Powell, William H. *The Fifth Army Corps*. New York: General Books LLC, 2010.

Quaife, Milo. *Letters from the Cannon's Mouth: The Civil War Letters of General Alpheus S. Williams*. Detroit, MI: Wayne State University Press, 1959.

Quint, Alonzo. *The Life and Letters of Wilder Dwight*. Boston, MA: Ticknor and Fields, 1891.

Sawyer, Franklin. *A Military History of the Eighth Regiment Ohio Volunteers*. Cleveland, Ohio, 1861.

Scharff, Thomas S. *A History of Western Maryland*. Philadelphia, PA: Lippincott, 1882.

Schildt, John W. *Doctor in Gray: Hunter Holmes McGuire*. Hagerstown, MD: Hagerstown Bookbinding, 1986.

———. *Four Days in October*. Hagerstown, MD: Hagerstown Bookbinding, 1978.

————. *September Echoes: A Study of the Maryland Campaign of 1862.* Middletown, MD: Valley Register, 1960.

Slocum, C.E. *Life and Services of Major General Henry Warner Slocum.* College Station, TX: Southern Methodist University Press, 1913.

Southern Historical Society Papers (SHSP). Vol. 10. Richmond, Virginia.

Strother, David. *A Virginia Yankee in the Civil War.* Chapel Hill, NC: University of North Carolina Press, 1961.

De Trobriand, Regis. *Four Years with the Army of the Potomac.* Boston, MA: Ticknor, 1889.

Villard, Oswald Garrison. *John Brown: A Biography, Fifty Years After.* Charleston, SC: Nabu Press, 1909.

War of the Rebellion: A Compilation of the Official Records of the Union and Confederate Armies. 128 vols. Washington, D.C.: Government Printing Office, 1880–91.

Wentz, A. Ross. *The Lutheran Church in Frederick County, Maryland, 1738–1938.* Lancaster, Pennsylvania, 1939.

Worthington, Glenn H. *Fighting for Time.* Baltimore, MD: Day Printing Company, 1932.

INDEX

ABOUT THE AUTHOR

John W. Schildt grew up in Frederick County and has been a lifelong student of history. A graduate of Shepherd University, Shepherdstown, West Virginia, he has been a teacher, a pastor and a hospital chaplain. John is the author of nineteen books on the Civil War, including *September Echoes*, *Drums Along the Antietam*, *Roads to and from Gettysburg* and *Lincoln's Wartime Travels*. He has led Antietam battlefield tours for college, civic and military groups and has spoken at the Gettysburg Civil War Institute and Dr. James Robertson's Campaigning with Lee program. As a postwar member of the Twenty-ninth Division, he has led three tours of Normandy. John and his wife, Mary Ann, live in Sharpsburg.

Visit us at
www.historypress.net